Science
Experiments
You Can Eat

Science Experiments You Can Eat

by Vicki Cobb

Illustrated by Peter Lippman

A Harper Trophy Book

Harper & Row, Publishers

ACKNOWLEDGMENTS

The author extends heartfelt thanks to Ellie Haines for precipitating the inspiration that became this book and for being such a good friend; to Ellen Dank for her never-fail yogurt recipe; to Drake, Liza, and Jenny McFeely for helping test procedures; to Theo and Josh, my children, for letting me work; and to my husband, Edward, for his critical review of all stages of the manuscript and his cheerful acceptance of a diet of science experiments.

Library of Congress Cataloging in Publication Data
Cobb, Vicki.
    Science experiments you can eat.

    Summary: Experiments with food demonstrate various scientific principles and produce an eatable result. Includes fruit drinks, grape jelly, muffins, chop suey, yogurt, and junket.
    1. Science—Experiments—Juvenile literature. 2. Cookery—Juvenile literature. [1. Science—Experiments. 2. Cookery] I. Lippman, Peter, illus. II. Title.
Q164.C52   502'.8   71-151474

ISBN 0-06-446002-9 (pbk.)

TO PAULA WOLF, MY MOTHER,

FOR WHOM COOKING IS A FINE ART.

Contents

1
A Kitchen Laboratory

Your kitchen at home is a well-equipped laboratory. Like kitchens, laboratories have a supply of water for preparing solutions, studying reactions, cultivating specimens, and washing glassware. Laboratories must have a source of heat, like the burners on a stove, for speeding up reactions and sterilizing instruments. Many laboratories have refrigerators for storing chemicals that keep better at colder temperatures or for slowing down reactions. Measuring instruments for determining the amounts of different substances needed are found in both laboratories and kitchens.

People who work in laboratories and kitchens use their equipment in much the same way. Both cooks and scientists separate, measure, and heat different substances. Cooks and scientists work with chemicals, though to a cook sodium chloride is salt and tartaric acid is cream of tartar. Plants and animals are of interest to both cooks and scientists.

Scientists study nature in the laboratory to produce information for a variety of uses. Cooks work in kitchens to produce food that is nutritious and good to eat. The experiments in this book are designed to get you started being a scientist in your own kitchen. You will be experimenting with food to find out about nature and, in the process, you will also be preparing food. Sometimes you can eat your completed experiments. At other times, you can use your experiment in a recipe and see how it is a part of a dish that is good to eat.

EXPERIMENTING WITH FOOD

When you next sit down to a meal, try to figure out how all the things on your plate began. Most foods were alive or pro-

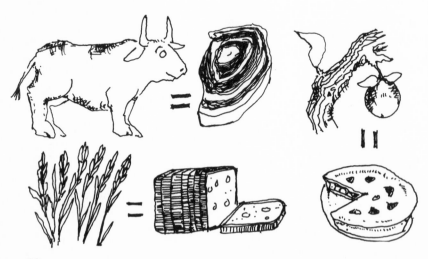

duced by a living thing at one time. Often the foods you eat have no resemblance to the animals and plants from which they came.

Many changes in food take place before it reaches your home. Some foods are prepared from only a part of a living thing, such as wheat germ, lard, and sugar. Foods may be processed so they will keep longer without spoiling. Chemicals are often added to breads and cakes to keep them moist and to crackers and potato chips to keep them dry and crisp. Fruits, vegetables, and meats are canned, dried, or frozen to keep harmful bacteria from making them unfit to eat. On the other hand, the growth of certain bacteria and other microorganisms is important in the preparation of foods such as bread, cheese, yogurt, and vinegar.

Cooking changes food still further. Heat makes some food softer and some food firmer. It changes the color of many foods. Different flavors blend when heated together. Heat destroys harmful bacteria and makes certain foods easier to digest.

It is easy to produce changes in food. Producing changes is what science is all about. If you can produce a change, you can learn something about the starting material from the way it changes.

All the experiments in this book are designed to show changes.

Sometimes the change is not great and you have to look closely to see if one has even occurred. When you know what you are looking for, even a small change can be very exciting. Every experiment has been tested but the materials you use and the conditions in your kitchen may be slightly different from those described in this book. If you don't get the expected results, try to think of what may be different in your laboratory. Try the experiment again in a different way to see if you can get expected results. Much of the scientist's time is spent in designing *procedures* or ways to do experiments. Good procedures give clear-cut results and are repeatable by anyone following the directions exactly.

HOW TO DO AN EXPERIMENT

To get the most out of this book you should know *what* you are doing in an experiment and *why* you are doing it. Every chapter has a short introduction that discusses the subject you will be investigating. Every experiment also has a short introduction that asks a question you can answer by doing the experiment.

To help you know what to do, materials and equipment for each experiment are listed. Collect everything before you begin a procedure. This way you will not be caught without something important at a critical time during the experiment.

The procedure section tells you how to do the experiment. Long or complicated procedures are stated step by step. Often, reasons for doing a certain step are discussed as you go along. Since timing is important, you should read and understand the procedure section before you try to do the experiment.

After the procedure there is a brief discussion of what your results mean. Questions in the book are to help you know what to look for in getting your results. They may also suggest follow-up experiments you can do with an experiment of your own design.

You will learn more if you do the experiments in the order in which they appear in this book. Often, understanding an experiment in a later chapter depends upon understanding experiments in earlier chapters.

There are certain standard procedures for safety and use of equipment for every laboratory, and your kitchen is not an exception. Consult the cook in your house before you start experimenting in your kitchen and ask about any procedures or terms you are not certain about.

2
Solutions

Scientists who study matter and changes in matter are called chemists. Matter is anything that has weight and takes up space; all things in the universe are made up of matter.

In nature, most matter is found mixed with other matter. There is, as you can imagine, almost no end to the kinds of mixtures. One of the most interesting kinds of mixtures is a solution. A sugar and water mixture is an example of a solution.

A solution is a special kind of mixture that is evenly mixed or *homogeneous*. A sample taken from the top will have exactly the same amounts of each substance as an equal sample taken from the bottom. You can understand how a solution is homogeneous if you think of matter as being made up of tiny particles, too

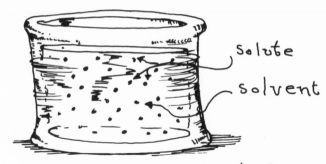

Solute
solvent

Homogeneous Mixture

small to see. When a mixture is homogeneous, the particles of one substance are evenly spread through the other. You can see this in the picture although of course particles of matter cannot be seen. This illustration is simply a model of a situation that cannot be seen.

There may be more than two substances in a solution, but solutions can be thought of as two *phases*. One phase is the *solvent* and the other is the *solute*. Each phase may have more than one component. The particles of the solvent are always touching each other. The particles of the solute are separated by the solvent particles. They may occasionally bump into each other but most of the time they remain apart as shown.

When a solute dissolves, the solute particles spread evenly through the solvent in a process called *diffusion*. You make a solution by putting a solute into a solvent; you don't even have to stir. Drop a lump of sugar (a solute) into a glass of water (a solvent) and let it stand for a while. What happens to the lump of sugar? When you can no longer see any sugar crystals, taste the solution with a straw. How can you tell that the sugar is still present? Use the straw to taste the top of the glass and the bottom. Is the solution homogeneous? How can you tell?

Solutions are important in the study of matter. You can often find out what a substance is by the solvent in which it dissolves and by how much of it will dissolve. Many chemical reactions take place in solutions that will not take place otherwise. The experiments in this chapter will introduce you to some different solutions and some of the ways solutions are used to learn about matter.

ROCK CANDY: RECOVERING SOLUTE CRYSTALS

It is not difficult to perform the reverse of making a sugar solution and separate the solvent from the solute. It is especially easy to recover the solute if you don't care about keeping the solvent. Leave a water solution open to the air and the solvent will evaporate and leave the solute behind. You can evaporate all kinds of solutions to see what was dissolved in them. Put a small amount of the solution in a shallow dish so that a large surface is exposed to the air.

Some solutes form crystals as the solvent evaporates. Crystals are solids that have a regular geometric shape, with many sides or faces. Some crystals of common substances are shown in the picture.

In this experiment you will be growing rock candy sugar crystals you can eat.

water, ½ cup

granulated sugar, 1 cup

a wooden spoon

a measuring cup

a small saucepan

some small shallow dishes (aluminum foil dishes work well)

PROCEDURE

Put the water in the pan. Put a spoonful of sugar in the water and stir. Use a wooden spoon so that the spoon handle won't get hot later on.

Continue to add a spoonful of sugar at a time, stirring after each addition until it dissolves. How many spoonfuls before the sugar stops dissolving no matter how much you stir? This solution is now said to be a *saturated* solution. Put a low flame under the saturated solution for a few minutes. Do the crystals dissolve when you heat the water?

Turn off the heat. Add sugar again, spoonful by spoonful to the hot solution. Does it take more sugar to make a saturated solution in hot water than it does in colder water? Pour all the remaining sugar from the measuring cup into the pan. Turn the flame on again and continue heating gently until all the sugar is dissolved. Bring it to the boiling point and boil for about a minute. The solution should be thick and clear and contain no sugar crystals. Pour the solution into the small dishes while it is hot.

Observations

Watch the solution as it cools. Be careful not to jolt it or disturb it in any way. Does the solution remain clear? If it becomes cloudy, take a close look at it with a magnifying glass. A clear solution that contains more solute than would normally dissolve at that temperature is said to be *supersaturated*. Supersaturated solutions are very unstable and the slightest disturbance will cause crystals to form, removing them from solution.

17

Some candy, like fudge, depends on the formation of millions of tiny crystals. Small crystals form quickly when you beat a supersaturated sugar solution. For rock candy, you want to grow large crystals. Large crystals grow slowly, over a period of weeks. Let the solution stand undisturbed at room temperature for a week or more. As water continues to evaporate, the solution will remain supersaturated and crystals will grow. After a few days, you might have to break and carefully remove the crust of crystals that forms at the surface so that water can continue to evaporate.

Rock candy crystals will form around any small object you put in the solution. Hang a weighted string in a glass of supersaturated sugar solution to see where crystals form. You can make rock candy lollipops by putting swizzle sticks in a glass of solution.

Crystals are interesting because they are a very pure form of matter and a clue to the structure of a substance. Scientists figure that the perfect shape of crystals is not an accident but is the result of a regular arrangement of particles too small to see. Matter

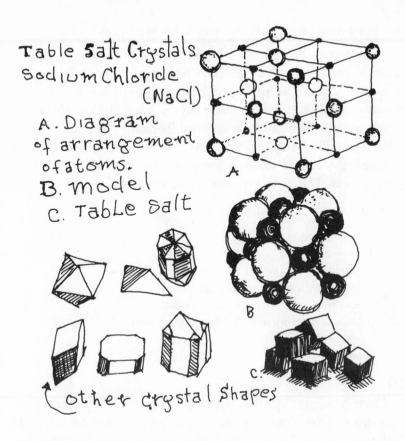

Table Salt Crystals
Sodium Chloride
                (NaCl)
A. Diagram
of arrangement
of atoms.
B. model
C. Table Salt

other crystal shapes

is made of particles, called *atoms* and *molecules*, that have a size and a shape. Crystals such as those in the illustration have been used to discover the size and shapes of many different atoms and molecules.

After you have grown some sugar crystals, compare them with crystals of granulated sugar. (Use a magnifying glass.) Are the crystals you have grown larger or smaller than granulated sugar? Are they the same shape? Do sugar crystals have the same shape as salt crystals? Do you think sugar molecules have the same shape as salt molecules?

19

ICE POPS AND THE FREEZING POINT OF SOLUTIONS

One question that comes up again and again in a laboratory is, How do you know when you have a pure substance? One way to answer this question is to see if a substance you know to be pure (usually because a manufacturer says so) acts differently from a substance you know to be a mixture (because you made it yourself). It is well established that pure water becomes a solid at 32° Fahrenheit. Does a solution freeze at the same temperature as pure water? The next experiment should give you the answer.

MATERIALS AND EQUIPMENT

2 measuring cups
6 five-ounce paper cups
6 circles of cardboard to cover the cups
6 swizzle sticks or wooden sticks
a pen that can write on paper cups
1 cup of a *clear*, not cloudy, canned fruit juice (cherry or grape)
water

PROCEDURE

When you set up this experiment you will put different amounts of fruit juice in each ice pop in a systematic way. The first ice pop will be undiluted fruit juice as it comes from the can, the second will be ½ fruit juice and ½ water, the third will by ¼ fruit juice and ¾ water, and so on. Such a systematic way of changing the amount of water is called *serial dilutions*. Serial dilutions are often used to test the strength of a substance; for example, to find out how much detergent to put in a washing machine and how much aspirin to take when you are sick.

Since the freezing of the ice pops is to be compared to the freezing of pure water, you will be making an ice pop that is only water, without juice. This ice pop is the *control*. A control is a part of an experiment that is treated just like every other part except that it does not contain the thing you are changing.

Mark the cups as shown in the illustration: Juice, ½, ¼, ⅛, ¹⁄₁₆, control.

Make sure that each cardboard circle covers the top of each cup without falling in. The purpose of the cover is to hold each stick upright until the ice pop has frozen. Punch a hole just large enough to insert a stick in the center of each cardboard circle. Place a stick in each hole.

Measure ½ cup of water and pour it into the cup marked "control."

Measure out 1 cup of juice. Use the second measuring cup to measure out ½ cup of juice from the first measuring cup. Pour ½ cup of juice into the paper cup labeled "juice."

Add just enough water to the remaining ½ cup juice in the measuring cup to bring the volume up to 1 cup. Mix well. Use the second measuring cup to get ½ cup of this dilution. Pour into the cup marked "½."

Add enough water to ½ cup of the first dilution to again bring

21

the volume up to 1 cup. Mix and use ½ cup of this mixture to make the next ice pop in the cup labeled "¼."

Follow the same procedure to make ice pops that are ⅛ juice and ¹⁄₁₆ juice.

Put the covers and sticks on each cup. Adjust the sticks so they just touch the bottom of the cups.

Put all six cups in your freezer. It is important to place them at the same depth so they will all be at the same temperature. After about 40 minutes, check to see how freezing is progressing by jiggling each stick back and forth. As freezing occurs you can feel the ice forming. Keep checking about every 20 minutes. Which ice pop freezes first? Which ice pop takes longest to freeze? Does it require more or less cold to freeze a solution?

Observations

On the basis of your experiment, why is salt put on sidewalks in winter? Why is alcohol put in car radiators before the cold weather sets in? How can the temperature at which something freezes be used to tell how pure a substance is?

When the ice pops are frozen solid, which may take several hours, your experiment is completed and you may eat them. Although some of the ice pops will taste better than others, even the control can be refreshing on a hot day. Just tear off the paper cup and enjoy!

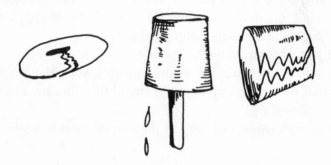

FRUIT DRINKS AND DISSOLVING RATES

If you have ever made beverages by dissolving solutes in water, you may have noticed that some solutes seem to dissolve faster than others. What causes some solutions to form more quickly than others? Does temperature have an effect on the rate at which a solvent goes into solution?

MATERIALS AND EQUIPMENT

3 small, colorless, clear glass tumblers
a measuring cup
boiling water, ice water, and water at room temperature
a package of unsweetened grape Kool-Aid

PROCEDURE

Put ½ cup of ice water in the first glass, ½ cup of water at room temperature in the second glass, and ½ cup of boiling water in the third glass.

Drop a few grains (a small pinch) of Kool-Aid into each glass. Watch how the Kool-Aid diffuses into solution.

Observations

In which glass does it dissolve most quickly? How long does it take for the Kool-Aid to diffuse evenly through the water?

Try this experiment with other colored solutes like instant coffee and cocoa.

After you have finished the experiment you can prepare Kool-Aid to drink. Pour all the solutions into a pitcher. Add the remaining Kool-Aid and the amount of sugar suggested on the package. Add 6½ cups of cold water to bring the volume up to two quarts.

SOUR-BALL ADE

Does the amount of surface area of the solute affect the rate at which it dissolves in the solvent? Try the next experiment to find out!

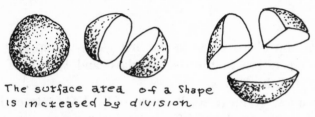

The surface area of a shape is increased by division

MATERIALS AND EQUIPMENT

3 pieces of dark-colored hard candy (grape or cherry)
3 small glasses
a measuring cup
waxed paper
a hammer or rolling pin
water at room temperature

PROCEDURE

Put ¼ cup of water into each glass. Wrap a candy in waxed paper and tap it lightly with the hammer or rolling pin so it breaks into several large pieces. Wrap another candy in waxed paper and smash it so it is like granulated sugar. Drop the whole candy into the first glass, the broken candy into the second glass, and the smashed candy into the third glass.

Observations

Which candy had the most surface area? Which candy dissolves first? How do you think the amount of surface area affects the rate at which a solute dissolves? How do your findings explain why superfine sugar is used to sweeten iced drinks?

You can make a refreshing drink from this experiment. Pour all three solutions into one glass and add a few ice cubes. An orange slice adds a festive touch.

RED CABBAGE INDICATOR

Two kinds of solutions that are especially interesting are *acids* and *bases*. Acids and bases have many fascinating properties, one of which is that of conducting electricity. The bulb in the illustration will light up when the electrodes are immersed in an acid or base.

Many foods we eat contain acid which gives food a sour taste. Lemon juice and vinegar are good examples of acids we eat. We also eat certain bases, although they are not as common as acids. Baking soda, for example, is a base when it is dissolved in water.

There are, of course, many stronger acids and bases which we don't eat because they are poisonous. Tasting is not a test used to determine an acid. A dye, called an *indicator*, is used to tell if a solution is acid or basic.

The color of an indicator changes depending on whether it is in an acid or a base. Litmus paper has been dipped in an indicator and dried. You can tell what a solution is by putting a few drops on litmus paper and watching the color change.

The pigment that makes red cabbage red can be used as an indicator. Here's how you do it:

MATERIALS AND EQUIPMENT

a red cabbage

water

2 bowls

a grater

a strainer

a slotted spoon

a knife

a very clean glass jar and cover

PROCEDURE

Cut the cabbage into quarters. Grate it section by section into a bowl. Add between one and two cups of water, depending on the size of the cabbage. Let the cabbage stand in the water, stirring occasionally so that all the cabbage is moistened.

When the water is a strong red, remove as much of the grated cabbage as you can with a slotted spoon. Pour the water solution through the strainer into the glass jar. Add the drained cabbage to the rest of the cabbage you have removed.

Put about a tablespoon of indicator into a small, white dish. Test a substance you know to be an acid and one you know to be a base first so that you can see the proper color changes. Here are some foods you can test:

1. cooking water from boiled vegetables, including beans, peas, onions, carrots, turnips, celery, asparagus, etc.
2. liquids from canned vegetables and fruits
3. cream of tartar
4. soda pop
5. egg white
6. fruit juices
7. tomato
8. cottage cheese

The grated red cabbage can be used for a salad or it can be cooked in a covered pot with a small amount of water. You can divide the cabbage in half, putting each half in an aluminum pot. Put a cut-up tart apple in only one pot. Use enough water to just cover the bottom of the pot ($\frac{1}{2}$–$\frac{1}{4}$ cup).

Observations

Which cooked cabbage is redder? Why? How do your findings support the idea that small amounts of aluminum combine with water to form aluminum hydroxide, a base?

Mix all the cooked cabbage together and season with salt, pepper, and butter to serve.

3
Suspensions, Colloids, and Emulsions

There are many kinds of matter that do not dissolve in water. Some mixtures, such as mud and water, contain particles that are heavy enough to settle to the bottom after being stirred up. This kind of mixture is called a *suspension* because the material is only suspended temporarily in the liquid. Separate the liquid from the large solid particles in a suspension by letting the particles settle and then by pouring off the liquid as shown in the illustration. This method of separation is called *decanting*.

If a suspension contains very small particles, it may take days or weeks to settle. Such a mixture cannot be separated by decanting but can be separated by pouring it through a strainer or filter. Filtering is used to determine the size of particles in a suspension as well as to separate solids from liquids.

Do the next experiment to learn more about suspensions and the way they are handled in a laboratory.

BORSCHT COCKTAIL: SEPARATING SUSPENDED PARTICLES

One kind of food suspension is called a *puree*. Purees are made by pushing soft food through a strainer or food mill so that it is broken up into very small particles. Pureed food is often mixed with liquid. Usually the food particles are so small that they take a long time to settle. Split pea soup, tomato sauce, and applesauce are examples of purees.

MATERIALS AND EQUIPMENT

a jar of borscht (beet soup)   2 glass jars
a strainer   a large spoon
some coffee filters   a watch with a second hand

Shake the jar of borscht. Use the watch to time how long it takes for the beet particles to settle to the bottom. Do some beet particles stay suspended longer than others? Which ones stay suspended longer?

Decant about a cup of the liquid off the top. Pour it through a strainer into a glass jar.

Observations

Are any beet particles caught by the strainer? What is the size of particles that pass through the strainer? Are they smaller or larger than the holes in the strainer?

PROCEDURE

Rinse out the strainer. Put a coffee filter in the bottom of the strainer and place it over the second glass jar. Pour the liquid you have just strained from the first glass jar into the filter paper and let the mixture drip through.

Observations

Are there any beet particles on the filter paper? Are these particles smaller or larger than the holes in the filter paper?

Taste the liquid that you have just filtered. How can you tell if there is sugar in borscht? (Confirm your findings by reading the list of ingredients on the label.) Is the size of sugar particles smaller or larger than the holes in the filter?

PROCEDURE

Remove the filter paper from the strainer. Take about two large spoonfuls of beets from the bottom of the jar of borscht. Push them through the strainer with a spoon into the liquid in the glass jar. Be sure to scrape the beets off the outside of the strainer. You can use some liquid in the jar to wash the pureed beets through the strainer.

Stir or shake the pureed beets into the liquid.

Observations

How long does it take these particles to settle? Do they all settle eventually? How does the settling time compare with the time for the pieces of beet before they were pureed? (If you find it difficult to see the beets, work in front of a strong light.)

From the results of your experiment, can you explain how settling rates and filtering can be used to find the size of particles? Can you think of how these procedures can be used to identify different substances as well as to separate them?

You can make a delicious cold soup with your experiment. Chill the pureed mixture. Beat in about a tablespoon of sour cream with a rotary egg beater.

LIQUID FOOD AND THE TYNDALL EFFECT

Solutions and suspensions are both mixtures with two phases. The main difference is the size of the particles of the solute phase. In a solution, solute particles are approximately the size of molecules. In a suspension, the particles are large enough to be filterable.

There is a third kind of mixture with two phases, called a *colloid*. Particles in a colloid are larger than molecules but small enough to remain in suspension permanently and be homogeneous. It is hard to tell the difference between a colloid and a solution by looking at them. There is, however, a simple test that does tell the difference. All you need is a glass tumbler and a flashlight.

The particles in a colloid are large enough to act as tiny mirrors and reflect light. If you pass a beam of light through a colloid you can see the beam. This ability to scatter light is called the *Tyndall effect*. You can see the Tyndall effect in a beam of sunlight in a dusty room or coming from car headlights on a foggy night. Fog and dust are large enough to reflect light while air molecules are too small.

The Tyndall effect can be demonstrated with liquids we eat. Pour a small sample of the liquid into a clear glass. Hold the glass against a dark background and shine a flashlight beam through it. (A pen flashlight works especially well.) Look at the beam from the side. If you can see the beam as it passes through,

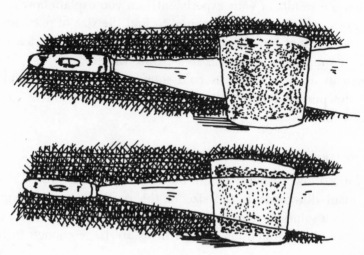

the liquid is a colloid. If you can't see the beam from the side, the liquid is a solution.

Which of the liquids listed are colloids and which are solutions: tea; cranberry juice; syrup (colorless); orange drink; coffee; salt water; gelatin dessert; Kool-Aid; consommé; vinegar (distilled); egg white; cider.

Protoplasm, the living material of all cells, is a complicated colloid. What would you expect if you shined a beam of light through protoplasm?

SALAD DRESSING: A LIQUID SUSPENDED IN A LIQUID

Among the different kinds of matter that do not mix with water are some liquids. Two liquids such as oil and water, that do not mix, will separate into layers if you shake them together and let them stand. Liquids that do not form solutions are said to be *immiscible*.

French salad dressing is a mixture of oil and vinegar and seasoning. Vinegar is a water-based substance and is immiscible with oil. In order for all the flavors of French dressing to be evenly spread through a salad, it must be thoroughly mixed. French dressing is usually given a number of hard shakes and is immediately poured on the salad before the two liquids have a chance to separate.

This experiment is designed to answer the question: Does the size of the droplets of two immiscible liquids affect the rate of separation into layers?

a jar with a tight cover
a small bowl
an egg beater
a watch or clock with a second hand
a magnifying glass

⅓ cup vinegar
⅔ cup salad oil
¼ teaspoon pepper
¼ teaspoon garlic powder
¼ teaspoon paprika
½ teaspoon salt

PROCEDURE

Put the vinegar in the jar and add the salt, pepper, garlic powder, and paprika. Cover the jar and shake. Pour in the oil and let the mixture stand for a few minutes.

Observations

Where does the oil go? What do you think would weigh more, a cup of water or a cup of oil? Can you think of a way to check your guess?

Cover the jar and shake about ten times. Use the watch to see how long it takes for the mixture to separate.

Shake the jar hard about twenty times. Does the dressing take more or less time to separate? Look for droplets of vinegar suspended in the oil.

Shake the jar different numbers of times and examine the size of the droplets immediately after shaking. When does the dressing have the smallest droplets?

Put the mixture in a small bowl and beat hard for about four minutes. Quickly pour the dressing back into the jar. Examine the droplets with a magnifying glass. How long does the dressing

34

take to separate into two layers? What did shaking and beating do to the size of the droplets?

You can use the French dressing over a tossed green salad. Mix well and use just enough to coat the leaves lightly.

When milk is homogenized, it is forced through tiny holes in a screen. This breaks up the butterfat in milk into very tiny droplets. In nonhomogenized milk, the fat rises to the top as cream. Why doesn't the fat separate from milk when it is homogenized?

MAYONNAISE: A STABILIZED SUSPENSION

When oil and vinegar in French dressing separate, the oil droplets grow larger and larger until they come together to form a separate layer. The addition of certain third substances to such a mixture of oil and water, prevents the oil droplets from coming together. If the oil droplets are kept from coming together, there is no separation into layers. The result is a stable mixture of two immiscible liquids called an *emulsion*. The substance that keeps the liquids apart is called an *emulsifying agent*.

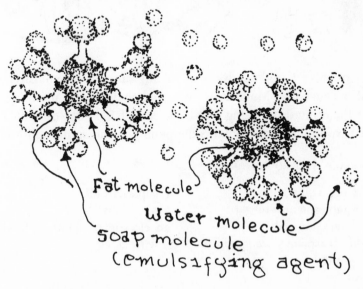

Fat molecule
Water molecule
Soap molecule
(emulsifying agent)

One example of an emulsifying agent is soap. When you wash greasy dishes, hot water turns the grease into an oil and the soap emulsifies the grease so it can be washed down the drain. Try washing greasy dishes in cold water with soap or in hot water without soap. Can you get the dishes clean?

Mayonnaise is an emulsion of oil in water. The emulsifying agent is egg yolks. Mayonnaise is a real challenge to many who pride themselves on being good cooks, but it is not difficult to make if you understand what is happening as the emulsion forms.

MATERIALS AND EQUIPMENT

2 egg yolks
3 tablespoons vinegar
½ teaspoon salt
¼ teaspoon prepared mustard

1 cup salad oil
a small bowl
an electric beater or a friend with an egg beater

Have all the ingredients at room temperature. Cold oil does not flow as quickly as warmer oil and cold egg yolks will not emulsify as much oil as warmer egg yolks. (Can you think of experiments to check these ideas out?)

Put the egg yolks, mustard, salt, and 1 teaspoon of vinegar in the bowl and beat at a medium speed until the egg yolks are sticky. The egg yolks are now thoroughly mixed with the water in the vinegar and are ready to receive the oil.

Add the oil drop by drop while beating constantly. If you do not have an electric beater, you can make the emulsion by hand with a friend. One of you does the beating with a rotary egg beater while the other adds oil.

The idea in making mayonnaise is to spread tiny droplets of oil evenly through the egg yolks. Egg yolk coats these droplets as they form and prevents them from coming together and forming a separate layer, as in the illustration. If you add the oil too fast, or too much oil at one time, the droplets will come together before they can be forced into the egg yolks and the mayonnaise will "curdle" or separate. If this happens, you can correct the situation with a fresh egg yolk, but add the curdled mayonnaise to the yolk rather than the oil.

You can tell when the emulsion has formed because the mixture gets thick. This usually happens after about ⅓ of a cup of oil has been added. Once the emulsion has formed, you can add the oil slightly faster until the full cup has been beaten into the yolks. If the mixture gets too thick, add a teaspoon of vinegar. Beat in the remaining vinegar at the end.

Homemade mayonnaise is thick, yellow, and glistening. It spoils easily and should be stored in the refrigerator. Cover it so a skin doesn't form on top.

Several cookbooks make the claim that mayonnaise is difficult to make on a rainy day or when a thunderstorm is threatening.

But mayonnaise is made commercially on every working day regardless of the weather. You might want to do some experiments to check this out.

STRAWBERRY BOMBE: A FROZEN EMULSION

Ice cream, bombes, and other frozen desserts contain water and cream. Separation of the fat in cream is not a problem because the fat droplets are very small. In frozen desserts the problem is to keep the water droplets small. Large water droplets form large ice crystals and give the dessert a grainy texture. As long as the ice crystals are tiny, the dessert will be smooth.

Suppose an emulsifying agent that attracts water is added to a frozen dessert. Do you think it can keep large ice crystals from forming as egg yolk kept large oil droplets from forming? You can find out when you make a strawberry bombe in the next experiment.

MATERIALS AND EQUIPMENT

1 package defrosted frozen strawberries
1 teaspoon unflavored gelatin
1½ tablespoons cold water
1½ tablespoons boiling water
3 tablespoons cold water
1 cup sugar
2 teaspoons lemon juice
2 cups heavy whipping cream

a small dish or cup
3 small bowls
2 pint-sized containers (plastic ice-cream containers are good)
a spoon
rubber spatula
rotary egg beater or electric mixer

Put the gelatin in the small dish or cup and add 1½ table-spoons cold water. Does the gelatin attract water? How can you tell? You may have to wait a few minutes before you can answer these questions.

Put the strawberries in one of the bowls and add the sugar and lemon juice. Mix well and put half the strawberry mixture in a second bowl.

When the gelatin has softened and absorbed all the cold water, add 1½ tablespoons of boiling water and stir until all the gelatin dissolves. Add the gelatin mixture to one of the strawberry mixtures and stir well. Add 3 tablespoons cold water to the other strawberry mixture as a control. Label the bowls so you know which one contains the gelatin.

Refrigerate the strawberry mixtures until the gelatin starts to thicken. It should not be firm but only slightly gelled.

When the gelatin mixture is ready, whip the cream so it stands in soft peaks. Put half the whipped cream into each strawberry mixture.

Gently combine the strawberries and cream by using a rubber spatula to bring the mixture from the bottom of the bowl to the top. Repeat the motion again and again until well mixed. Wet the containers by rinsing with water. Put some dessert in each mold. Be sure to label the one containing the gelatin. Put the molds in the freezer for about 12 hours. When the desserts are frozen, taste them.

Observations

Is there a difference in texture between the one containing gelatin and the one without?

Let a few tablespoons of each dessert thaw and then refreeze them. Which dessert has a grainier texture? What do you think the gelatin does in a strawberry bombe?

4
Carbohydrates and Fats

Up to this point you have been experimenting with mixtures. Mixtures are made up of many different substances that can be purified. There are only two kinds of pure substances, compounds and elements.

Elements are the simplest kinds of pure matter. There are 92 elements which can be found in the earth's crust and a number of other elements which have been made in laboratories. The most common elements found in food (and the elements of which you are made) are carbon, hydrogen, oxygen, and nitrogen. Living things also contain sulfur, phosphorus, iron, magnesium, sodium, and chlorine, to name a few.

It took a long time to discover all of the elements. This is because elements combine to form compounds, another kind of pure matter. It was hard to tell when a pure substance was an element and when it was a compound. For a long time, water was thought to be an element. It was a great scientific breakthrough when water was found to be a compound made of hydrogen and oxygen, two substances known to be elements.

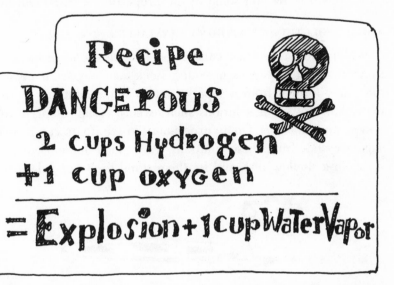

Recipe

DANGEROUS

2 cups Hydrogen
+1 cup oxygen

= Explosion + 1 cup Water Vapor

Elements combine to form compounds very differently from the way substances combine to form mixtures. Usually a compound has very different properties from the elements that make it, as shown in the illustration. (Can you think how water is different from oxygen and hydrogen?) Elements also combine in fixed amounts to form compounds. Any amount of hydrogen and oxygen can be mixed together but water forms from two volumes of hydrogen and one of oxygen. Any extra hydrogen or oxygen will be left over after water has formed.

Sugars and starches are compounds that are an important kind of food. Sugars and starches are made of only three elements—carbon, hydrogen, and oxygen. When sugars and starches are broken down to these elements, there are two atoms of hydrogen and one of oxygen for every atom of carbon. Two atoms of hydrogen and one atom of oxygen are the same as a molecule of water. For this reason, sugars and starches were called *carbohydrates* which means "watered carbon." The experiments in this chapter will show you some of the properties of carbohydrates.

SYRUPS: SOLUTIONS THAT DON'T CRYSTALLIZE

When you made rock candy you saw that one property of sugar is that it dissolves in water. Rock candy is sugar crystals that have formed from a supersaturated sugar solution. We use many kinds of sugar solutions such as corn syrup, maple syrup, honey, and molasses. Do an experiment to see if you can recover sugar crystals from these solutions. Pour small amounts of each syrup in a shallow dish and let them stand for several days.

In some cases, no crystals will form and you will be left with a thick sticky material in each dish. This raises a question you can answer with experiments: Does sugar absorb water from the air while water is evaporating so that most of the sugar remains in solution?

You can test this idea by making a supersaturated sugar solution as for rock candy (Chapter 2). Divide the solution into two dishes. Leave one dish exposed to the air and cover the other with a cake cover. Before you cover the second dish, sprinkle some calcium chloride on the table around it. Calcium chloride absorbs moisture from the air and will keep the air above the dish dry. You can get calcium chloride in hobby shops.

Do crystals form more slowly from a solution containing several solutes than a solution containing only one solute?

MATERIALS AND EQUIPMENT

½ cup water
⅔ cup sugar
2½ tablespoons white corn syrup
¼ teaspoon cream of tartar

a saucepan with a cover
a candy thermometer
a spoon
3 aluminum dishes

PROCEDURE

Put all the ingredients in the saucepan and stir until dissolved. When the mixture starts to boil, cover it briefly so that the steam washes all the sugar crystals on the side of the pan back into the solution. Uncover and put in the candy thermometer. Continue to boil without stirring until the temperature is 290° Fahrenheit. Pour into a foil dish.

Repeat the procedure with new ingredients twice. One time leave out the cream of tartar and the other time heat it only until all the sugar is dissolved. As the solutions cool, you can tell when crystals have formed because the solution becomes cloudy. Close examination with a magnifying glass will reveal thousands of tiny, needlelike crystals. Where do crystals form? They should form in two of the syrup batches while one should remain clear.

There are a number of different kinds of sugars. All are sweet and they all dissolve in water. Some sugars contain only five or six carbon atoms per molecule. These are called simple sugars and they include glucose (sometimes called dextrose) from beets, fructose from fruit, and lactose from milk. Table sugar is called sucrose. It is not a simple sugar because each molecule is a two-molecule chain of fructose and glucose.

When a sucrose solution is heated to a high temperature, it begins to break down into glucose and fructose. This breakdown is speeded up with the addition of an acid such as cream of tartar. The result is a syrup containing a mixture of three sugar solutes —glucose, fructose, and sucrose. Crystals will not form in such a mixture because a crystal is the result of the regular arrangement of identical molecules. When there are many different kinds of molecules in a solution, similar molecules have a hard time getting together, as in the illustration.

The syrups you have made can be used over ice cream or popcorn.

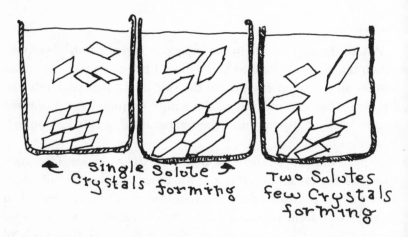

single Solute →
← Crystals forming

Two Solutes
few Crystals
forming

HYGROSCOPIC COOKIES

If you are a cookie eater, you may have noticed that cookies lose their crispness when they have been exposed to the air for a while. This is one reason why cookie manufacturers package their products to keep them from exposure to water vapor in the air. The ingredient in cookies that is chiefly responsible for absorbing moisture is sugar. Such a substance is called *hygroscopic* which means "wet looking."

Is one kind of sugar more hygroscopic than another? The next experiment compares cookies made with granulated sucrose with those made with honey. Taste honey and sugar. Which is sweeter? The procedure has been adjusted for differences in sweetness and amount of water.

MATERIALS AND EQUIPMENT

flour	a flour sifter
sugar	electric mixer or egg beater
honey	measuring cups
1 egg	measuring spoons
double-acting baking powder	4 bowls
unsalted butter	rubber spatula
salt	waxed paper
lemon juice	metal spatula
	a baking sheet

PROCEDURE

Preheat the oven to 400°F. Sift 2 cups of flour onto waxed paper. Measure out 1 cup of flour and resift it into a bowl with ½ teaspoon baking powder and ½ teaspoon salt.

Sift a second cup of sifted flour with ½ teaspoon baking powder and ¼ teaspoon salt into a second bowl. Set dry ingredients aside.

Put ½ bar of unsalted butter into a third bowl. Beat until creamy with an electric mixer or rotary egg beater.

Add ½ cup of sugar to the butter and continue beating until thoroughly mixed.

Beat the egg with a fork in a measuring cup. Put half the egg into the butter-sugar mixture. Add one bowl of dry ingredients with two tablespoons of water and ½ teaspoon lemon juice. Blend until smooth.

Now prepare the batter with honey. Put ½ bar of butter in a fourth bowl and beat until creamy. Beat in ¼ cup honey. Add the other half of the egg and the second bowl of dry ingredients to the butter-honey mixture. Leave out the lemon juice as honey contains an acid. Mix until well blended.

Drop the cookies by level teaspoons on greased cookie sheets. Bake until brown around the edges, about 7 minutes. Be sure to keep track of which cookies contain sugar and which contain honey.

Let the cookies cool for a few minutes until they can be moved to a plate with a metal spatula. Store the cookies in a closed container.

Observations

Eat a sugar cookie and a honey cookie when they are cool. Are they about the same crispness? Are they the same color? Which are browner? Leave one of each kind of cookie exposed to the air. Take a bite of each every few hours. Which cookie loses its crispness most quickly? If you wanted to make a cake that would stay moist for a long time, what might you use to keep it moist?

STARCHES

Starch is made by plants and animals as a way of storing sugars. A starch molecule is made of long chains of sugar molecules. It can easily be changed back to sugar when needed. If you have any doubt that starch is made of sugar, you can prove it for yourself with a simple experiment.

A STARCH MOLECULE

A soda cracker is made of flour (a starch), water, and baking powder. It contains no sugar. Chew a soda cracker well and hold it in your mouth for 5 minutes. Does the taste of the soda cracker change? There is a special chemical in your saliva that breaks the links in the starch chains so that sugar molecules are released. You should be able to taste this change.

Compare other properties of starches and sugars. How is the taste different? Try putting different starches in water. You can use cornstarch, potato starch, arrowroot starch, and flour. Which dissolves most easily? In general, larger molecules such as starch do not dissolve as easily as smaller molecules such as sugar.

Like sugar, starches also absorb water. When starches are heated with water, they swell and increase in size. This property makes them very useful as thickeners for sauces and gravies.

Many different foods contain starch. You can find out which ones have starch with a simple test. Put a few drops of iodine solution from your medicine chest on the food. If starch is present the iodine changes from reddish-brown to a blue-black. *Don't eat any food on which you put iodine! Iodine is poisonous.* Be sure to put the iodine away when you have finished.

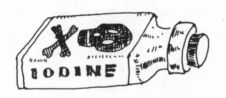

TAPIOCA

Tapioca is a starch that comes from the root of a Brazilian cassava plant. It is sold as dried "pearls" that can be used to make thick puddings.

Put a drop of iodine on a tapioca pearl. Does it give a positive starch test? Discard the pearl you tested. Take ¼ cup of tapioca

Cassava Roots

pearls and put them in ¾ cup of water. Let them soak for 12 hours. How does the size of the soaked tapioca compare with dried pearls? How is this evidence that starches swell with water?

Make tapioca pudding with the soaked pearls.

MATERIALS AND EQUIPMENT

soaked tapioca pearls	a double boiler
2¼ cups milk	4 dessert cups
¼ teaspoon salt	a wooden spoon
2 eggs	a measuring cup
½ cup sugar	an egg beater
1 teaspoon vanilla	

PROCEDURE

Test a small sample of milk, salt, eggs, sugar, and vanilla for starch. *Don't use any ingredients you have tested in preparing the pudding.* Is starch present in any of these ingredients?

Put the soaked pearls in the top of the double boiler with milk and salt. Cook, uncovered, over boiling water for about an hour, stirring occasionally with the wooden spoon.

Beat the eggs with the sugar. Mix a few spoonfuls of the hot tapioca mixture into the egg-sugar mixture.

Add the egg-sugar mixture to the tapioca in the pot. Cook about 3 minutes more.

Cool for 15 minutes, then mix in the vanilla. Pour into dessert dishes, cool and chill.

Test part of the pudding (not a pearl) for starch. Wash off a pearl from the pudding and test it for starch. What has happened to some of the starch that was in the tapioca pearls? What has this starch done to the liquid milk? Again, *don't eat* anything that has iodine on it.

GRAPE JELLY: HOW PECTIN ACTS

Pectin is a starch found in especially high amounts in green apples and the white underskin of citrus fruits. When pectin is cooked with sugar and acid, it swells to form a clear, thick jelly.

Pectin is prepared commercially and packed with an acid. It is an ideal material to find out if sugar, in addition to pectin and acid, is necessary for the formation of a firm jelly. This is what the next experiment is about.

MATERIALS AND EQUIPMENT

1 package of SURE-JELL (commercially prepared pectin and acid)
1 six-ounce can of grape concentrate (thawed)
sugar
water

a large saucepan
4 six-ounce glasses or jelly jars
a metal spoon
melted paraffin for sealing off the jelly (not necessary if all the jelly is eaten within two weeks)
measuring spoons
a measuring cup

Measure out 1 cup of sugar and set aside. Put 3 ounces of concentrate, 1 cup of water, and ½ package of Sure-Jell (2½ tablespoons) in the saucepan. Stir constantly over a high heat until bubbles form all around the edge.

Add the sugar. Bring the mixture to a boil and boil hard, while stirring, for one minute.

Remove from the heat. Use a spoon to skim off the top. Pour into two glasses. If you plan to store the jelly, cover the top with melted paraffin.

Make a second batch of jelly with the remaining Sure-Jell and concentrate. Use 1 cup of water and 2 cups of sugar.

Observations

Which jelly is firmer? The softer jelly can be used as a sauce over vanilla ice cream.

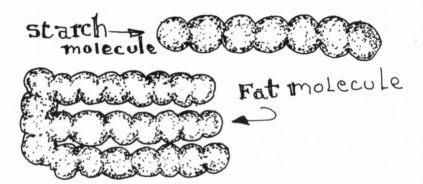

FATS

Most compounds found in living organisms are made up of only a few of the 92 naturally occurring elements. There are countless numbers of compounds made of only three elements: carbon, hydrogen, and oxygen. The differences between these compounds come from the amounts of each element in the compound and the ways the atoms are arranged in the molecules.

Fats are like carbohydrates in that they are another group of compounds made of only carbon, hydrogen, and oxygen. Fats are produced by animals and plants as a method of storing food. Molecules of sugars and starches become fat molecules as the atoms are rearranged. Fat protects an organism against a time when food is scarce.

You can find out if a food contains fat by rubbing it on a piece of brown paper bag. If the food contains fat, a translucent spot (an area that lets light through) will appear where you have rubbed. Water in food will also produce a translucent spot but a water spot disappears when the water dries. A fat spot will not disappear.

Animal fats, such as butter or lard, are usually solids at ordinary temperatures while vegetable fats are liquids. Vegetable oils can be made into solid fats in a laboratory by adding hydrogen gas under pressure. The terms "saturated" and "unsaturated" fats are another way of talking about the amount of hydrogen in a fat. Saturated fats contain more hydrogen than unsaturated or "polyunsaturated" fats. Saturated fats are usually solid while unsaturated fats are oils. Margarine, which is advertised as being made from oil, contains some saturated fat. Hydrogen has been added to some of the oil to make the fat solid.

These days, people are concerned with the kinds of fats they eat because different kinds of fats may affect health. As the human body ages, yellowish, fatty deposits of a substance called cholesterol form on the insides of blood vessels, causing them to become narrow. This condition, called arteriosclerosis, can cause blood clots which may block an artery and cause it to burst. If this happens to one of the arteries that brings blood to the heart or brain, death can result. Saturated fats in the diet seem to increase the amount of cholesterol in the body and unsaturated fats seem to lower blood-cholesterol levels. For this reason, doctors suggest that older people cut down on the amounts of butter and cheese and fatty meats in their diets.

NUT BUTTER: PRESSING OUT OILS

Many vegetable oils are prepared by crushing olives, seeds, or nuts in presses. The oil is then separated from the nut or seed from which it was pressed. You can release the oil in nuts in the next experiment. Since you cannot separate the oil easily, the mixture of oil and nuts produces a nut butter that is good to eat.

MATERIALS AND EQUIPMENT

½ to 1 cup shelled almonds,   a rolling pin
      pecans, or walnuts   a nut grinder
2 plastic bags

If you use pecans or walnuts there is no special preparation necessary before you crush them. Almonds should be white with the outer skins removed. You can remove almond skins by putting shelled almonds into boiling water for a few minutes. Drain them and let them cool. The almonds pop out of their skins if you hold them at the broad end and squeeze gently.

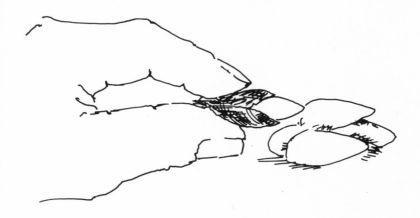

Put the nuts through a nut grinder or in a double plastic bag and pound with a rolling pin. Every once in awhile shake the bag so the nuts are rearranged.

After all the nuts are ground, put them into a plastic bag and roll the rolling pin on them with as much pressure as possible. (Hydraulic presses are used commercially to extract oil from olives and peanuts.) The nut particles will begin to cling together as the oil is pressed from the nut meat. The finer the nut meat, the better the butter will be. Store the nut butter, covered, in the refrigerator as it spoils easily.

Nut butters can be used as spreads on bread and crackers. Try a nut butter and jelly sandwich for a variation of an old favorite.

BUTTER: COALESCING FAT DROPLETS FROM A SUSPENSION

Milk has often been called the "most complete food." It contains water, carbohydrates, vitamins, minerals, proteins, and fat. Butter is made by extracting the fat from some of the other parts of milk. Since cream contains more butterfat than whole milk, you can see how butter is made from cream in the next experiment.

MATERIALS AND EQUIPMENT

½ pint heavy cream
a pint glass jar with a tight cover
a marble

PROCEDURE

Put the cream in the jar with the marble. Screw on the cover and make sure that no leaking can occur. Shake the jar in a figure-eight motion. At first you will hear the marble moving. Then there will be a time when the cream will be so thick that you won't be able to feel the marble moving. Then, all of a sudden, the butter will form. Drain the butter from the buttermilk—which is also good to drink—wash the butter with cold water to remove any trapped buttermilk, and pack down. Store in the refrigerator.

The process of making butter takes advantage of certain properties of fat. When milk first comes from a cow, the butterfat is in the form of droplets that are suspended in the mixture. If fresh whole milk is allowed to stand, fat droplets rise to the top, carrying along some liquid. This mixture is cream and is less dense than the other part of the milk.

Cream is a fat-in-water emulsion. This means that the fat droplets are held in suspension by milk protein. The buttermaking process is the formation of a water-in-fat emulsion. Here, water droplets are suspended by the fat, as in the illustration.

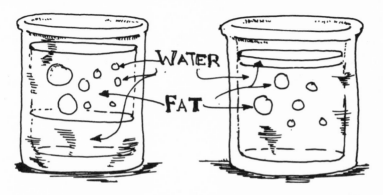

When you made butter from cream, you forced the fat droplets to come together. They formed larger and larger globules until they separated from the water part of the mixture. This process is called *coalescing*. Coalescing fat can happen because the fat globules are more attracted to each other than they are to the water in which they are suspended.

The amount of butterfat varies in cream. Light cream has much less butterfat than heavy cream. The amount of fat in cream is the most important factor in making good whipped cream. Try making whipped cream from heavy cream and light cream. Which whips most easily? Which keeps its stiffness longest?

5
Proteins

In the eighteenth century, scientists became interested in a kind of substance found in all living things that acted differently from all other substances. If a fluid like blood or egg white was heated, it did not become a boiling liquid like water or oil. Instead, it became a *solid*. And, if this was not strange enough, once changed to a solid, it could never again be a liquid. Nothing could be done to return blood or egg white to its original liquid state. It did not take scientists long to realize that this strange material that changed permanently when heated was the very basis of all life. For this reason, they named it "protein" meaning, "of first importance."

Proteins have turned out to be the most complicated and numerous of all the compounds found in living things. Some proteins, like egg white, dissolve in water; some, like hair, are fibers. Some, like muscle protein, are responsible for movement in animals. But all proteins have certain things in common. In addition to the elements carbon, hydrogen, and oxygen, all proteins also contain nitrogen. The atoms of these elements, along with an occasional atom of sulfur, form small molecules called *amino acids*. Proteins are chains of amino acids.

Only 20 different amino acids make up most proteins. These different amino acids are like our 26-letter alphabet. When you think of all you can say with 26 letters, you can see how 20 amino acids can be used to form so many different kinds of proteins.

When human beings and other animals digest their food, the protein is broken down into amino acids. This supply of amino acids is absorbed into the body and used to build new proteins. Every living organism forms its own particular brand of proteins from a supply of amino acids.

Scientists have found protein to be one of the most challenging kinds of material to study. You can use some of their methods of investigation to learn how different kinds of protein behave and how some of the properties of certain proteins are important in food preparation.

MERINGUES: THE PROPERTIES OF EGG WHITE

Egg white is a good place to start learning about proteins. It is made up of about 87 percent water, a trace of minerals, and about 9 percent protein. The protein in egg whites makes it very useful for preparing food with different textures and consistencies.

MATERIALS AND EQUIPMENT

3 eggs
water
a deep bowl
a small, transparent glass
a small plastic container with
    a cover

a flashlight
a spoon
an egg beater
a magnifying glass

Let the eggs come to room temperature. Protein in egg white is most useful to cooks at about 70°F. (You can check this out by trying to make meringues from egg whites at different temperatures.)

Separate the whites from the yolks. Use a knife to make a hard crack in the middle of each egg. Hold the cracked egg upright over the bowl as shown in the illustration and remove the top half of the shell. As the shell comes off, some of the white will slip into the bowl. To remove the rest of the white, gently transfer the yolk from one shell half to the other, letting the white slip out into the bowl. Be very careful not to let the yolk break and get mixed into any of the white. If you do, use the egg for scrambling or baking and begin again. You can store the yolks in a small container, covered in the refrigerator. The yolks can be used to make the mayonnaise in Chapter 3.)

Pour enough egg white into the glass to make a depth of two inches. Shine a beam of light through the egg white. Can you see the beam as it passes through? The beam is an example of the Tyndall effect. What does it tell you about the size of the particles in egg white? See Chapter 3 if you don't remember about the Tyndall effect. Protein particles have proven to be single molecules. They are among the largest molecules in existence.

Pour the egg white back into the bowl. Put some water in the glass. Take about a teaspoon of egg white and stir it into the water. Does the egg white dissolve?

Beat the egg white in the bowl with an electric beater or rotary egg beater until it is foamy but will still flow if poured. Take about ½ teaspoon of foam and put it in a fresh glass of water. Does it dissolve? What shape do the tiny particles have that are suspended in the water? Use a magnifying glass.

You have just demonstrated a very important property of proteins. That is, that the shape of a protein molecule plays an important part in determining how it behaves. Protein molecules in egg white are like tiny balls of yarn. Their round, compact shape enables them to dissolve in water. When you beat egg white, you are, in effect, unravelling these balls of yarn. The long chains which form are too large to dissolve. The process of changing protein from its natural form is called *denaturing*. It is impossible to restore denatured egg white to its original form.

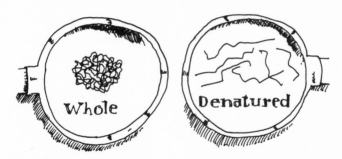

The egg white can be used to make meringues which show some other properties of proteins.

MATERIALS AND EQUIPMENT

¼ teaspoon cream of tartar   brown paper
¼ teaspoon salt   an egg beater
oil   measuring spoons
½ teaspoon vanilla extract   a rubber spatula
3 egg whites   a cookie sheet
1 cup superfine sugar

Preheat the oven to 175°F. Prepare a cookie sheet by covering it with oiled brown paper.

Add the cream of tartar, salt, and vanilla extract to the egg whites. Cream of tartar is an acid that makes the foam last longer.

(You can test this idea with a simple experiment. Beat two egg whites in separate bowls. Add ⅛ teaspoon cream of tartar to one egg white before you beat it. Find out which foam lasts longer.)

Beat the egg whites with an electric beater or rotary egg beater until you can make peaks that stand upright. As the egg white is beaten, the protein becomes more and more unraveled and the foam becomes stiffer and stiffer.

Slowly add the sugar by sprinkling a tablespoon at a time over the egg whites. Continue beating while adding the sugar. Occasionally scrape down the sides of the bowl with a rubber spatula.

The water in the egg whites is carried along the strands of protein. When sugar is beaten into stiff egg whites, it dissolves into this water. This is why you use superfine sugar (which dissolves more easily) and you add it very slowly to give it a chance to go into solution. If all the sugar doesn't dissolve, tiny droplets of sugar syrup will form on the surface of the finished product. Professional chefs consider such a "weeping" meringue a failure.

After you have added all the sugar, taste the meringue. It should not feel gritty but if it does, beat in a tablespoon of water to dissolve all the sugar.

Make four separate piles of meringue on the oiled paper. Push down the middle of each pile to make a bowl shape.

The last step in making a meringue is to remove the water. This is accomplished by drying it in a warm oven for a long time.

Put the meringues in the oven for one hour at 175°F. At the end of that time, turn off the oven and let the meringues stay in the oven overnight.

A successful meringue is a stiff, snow-white confection that will keep for weeks in a closed container. (Since sugar absorbs moisture from the air, meringues must be stored away from the air. Otherwise, they become soft and fall apart.)

Fill the meringues with fruit and top with whipped cream to serve.

CUSTARD: COAGULATING PROTEIN

The process of changing liquid protein into a solid by heating it is called *coagulation*. Coagulation is a kind of denaturing. Egg white coagulates at about 156°F. It changes from an almost colorless, transparent, fairly thick liquid to a white solid. The protein in egg yolk also coagulates when heated.

Protein coagulation is one of the main reasons food changes when it is cooked. Cooked meat and fish become firm and batters change from liquids to solids. In fact, most baked goods have a "skeleton" of coagulated milk and egg protein which supports them.

Custard is a homogeneous mixture of eggs, milk, and sugar that has been heated to coagulate the protein in eggs and milk. The purpose of the next experiment is to see how different amounts of heat affect the coagulation of these proteins.

MATERIALS AND EQUIPMENT

½ cup sugar
⅛ teaspoon salt
3 eggs
2 cups milk
1 teaspoon vanilla extract

4 custard cups or other oven-
    proof cups
a pan the cups will fit into
a bowl
an electric beater or rotary egg
    beater
measuring spoons and cups

PROCEDURE

Preheat the oven to 325°F. Beat the sugar, salt, and vanilla extract into the milk. Add the eggs and beat well.

Divide the mixture equally into four custard cups. Set the cups in the pan and cover the bottom of the pan with about an inch of water. (This is to make sure that the bottom of the cups are not heated more than any other part.) Put the custards in the oven for 30 minutes.

After 30 minutes, remove one cup of custard. Remove the next cup at 40 minutes, the third cup at 50 minutes, and the fourth cup at one hour.

Which custard has been properly cooked? Which custard separates from a watery liquid most easily?

When eggs first coagulate, the protein is able to trap and hold other liquids such as the water in the milk and egg whites. If eggs are cooked too long or at too high a temperature, they become tougher and tougher and can no longer hold water. Scrambled eggs, for example, from which water has separated have been either overcooked or cooked too quickly.

Properly made custard is a smooth, shiny, yellow pudding that slices cleanly when you put a spoon into it. There is no trace of water from either the egg or milk.

All custards are good to eat. The overcooked custards should be drained before eating. They can be topped with fruit.

SOUR MILK BISCUITS: PROTEIN DENATURED BY ACID

Some protein is easily denatured by acid. You can tell when this happens if solid particles form in a liquid that contains dissolved protein, like milk.

Have ½ cup of milk at room temperature. Put two teaspoons of vinegar, a weak acid, in another cup. Pour the milk into the vinegar and stir. Let the mixture stand for about 10 minutes. How can you tell if the protein is denatured? Stir the milk. Can you get the denatured protein to dissolve?

You can use the sour milk to make biscuits. Just substitute it for whole milk in a package of biscuit mix and follow the directions on the box.

If all protein were as easily denatured as that in eggs and milk, life could not survive. About 40 percent of the protein in our bodies and the bodies of other animals is considerably tougher than protein in eggs and milk. It already exists as a solid that will not dissolve in water. This protein, called *collagen,* is found in cartilege, the white, flexible material at the ends of bones. It is also found in tendons, which attach muscles to bones; ligaments, which tie bones together; and it is the main protein in bones themselves. Collagen is the protein that keeps us from falling apart.

As you might expect, collagen is also found in meat we eat. Tougher cuts of meat contain more collagen than more tender cuts. The problem in preparing tough meats is to make the collagen softer.

Fortunately, this is not a difficult task. When collagen is heated with water for a while, it breaks down into a smaller softer protein called *gelatin*. The process of changing collagen to gelatin is speeded up with the addition of an acid like lemon juice, vinegar, or tomatoes to the cooking water. (Some cooks soak or marinate tough meats in vinegar before stewing.) A tomato stew should become tender sooner than one made in meat broth alone. Can you design an experiment to confirm this?

If you would like to prepare almost pure gelatin, get two or three veal bones from your butcher. Veal bones, which come from young calves, have a great deal of cartilege. (As animals grow older, cartilege is replaced with bone.) Cover the veal bones with water and boil for an hour. Strain the broth and let it cool. You can improve the taste of the gelatin in the broth by adding tomato juice.

Gelatin is different from collagen. For one thing, gelatin dissolves in hot water while collagen doesn't dissolve at all. You can learn about some other properties of gelatin in the next experiment.

MATERIALS AND EQUIPMENT

a package of unflavored gelatin	a clear glass
	a flashlight
a package of Kool-Aid with sugar	a measuring cup
	a small pot
	a small bowl
	a two-cup mold

PROCEDURE

Sprinkle the package of gelatin on ½ cup of cold water. Does gelatin attract water? How can you tell?

When the gelatin has been softened, add 1½ cups of boiling water and stir. Does the gelatin dissolve? This mixture is called a "sol."

Taste the sol. Commercial gelatin is so tasteless that it can be used to make desserts as well as meat dishes.

Pour some of the sol into a clear glass. Shine a light through it. Does it show the Tyndall effect? What does this tell you about the size of gelatin molecules?

Let the sol cool, then chill it. The most dramatic property of gelatin is revealed when a sol cools. It changes from a liquid to a semisolid quivering mass called a "gel."

Observations

Shine a light through the gel. Does it show the same Tyndall effect as the sol? Is there any sign of water in the gel?

Put the gel in the pot and heat it. Can you reverse the change from sol to gel by adding heat? Add ½ package of Kool-Aid with sugar to the sol and stir until it is dissolved. Pour the flavored gelatin mixture into a mold, cool and chill until set.

You can unmold the set gelatin by changing the gel next to the mold back into a sol. Fill the sink with hot water and have a plate that covers the top of the mold ready. Put the mold into the water for about 10 seconds. Be careful not to let any water get on the gelatin. Put the plate over the mold, turn the whole thing over and give it a hard shake. You should hear the gelatin plop on the plate. If the gelatin doesn't slip out, heat it again for a few seconds and repeat the procedure. Be careful that you don't heat it too much as you can lose the sharp shape of the mold on your dessert.

A gelatin dessert can be unmolded long before it is to be

served. Just return it to the refrigerator until you are ready to eat it.

The sol-gel transformation has fascinated scientists. They have been curious about what happens to the water. Their research has shown that the water is trapped by a network of gelatin molecules that forms when gelatin cools. They have also found that as gelatin ages it is able to hold less and less water.

You can see how gelatin loses moisture with age by cutting some of your gelatin dessert into 1-inch cubes. Leaves the cubes on a plate in the refrigerator for several days. Every morning and evening eat a cube to see how they begin to get tougher as they get dryer.

MUFFINS: A STUDY OF GLUTEN—THE WHEAT PROTEIN

Denatured protein is the "skeleton" that supports baked products. In cakes and muffins and other delicate baked goods this support comes from coagulated milk and eggs. In bread, the support comes from a protein found in flour called *gluten*.

Wheat flour does not actually contain gluten. It contains two substances that can become gluten under the right conditions. The next experiment will show you some of the conditions needed to develop gluten and the effect of different amounts of gluten on the texture of muffins.

all-purpose flour
cake flour (not self-rising)
salt
butter
sugar
milk
baking powder
2 eggs

3 bowls
2 spoons
a small frying pan
paper muffin cups
an electric beater or rotary egg
    beater
a muffin tin
measuring cups and spoons
a flour sifter
waxed paper

PROCEDURE

Preheat the oven to 350°F. Put eight muffin cups in the muffin tin, four on each side so you make two groups separated by four empty cups in the center.

Sift about a cup of all-purpose flour on a sheet of waxed paper. All-purpose flour contains more protein that can become gluten than cake flour. Measure out 1 cup of this flour and resift it into a bowl with 1 tablespoon of sugar, ½ teaspoon of salt, and 1 teaspoon of baking powder. This mixture will be treated to develop the gluten.

Repeat the sifting of the flour, sugar, salt, and baking powder, only use a clean piece of waxed paper and use cake flour instead of all-purpose flour. Cake flour has a lower gluten content. This mixture will be treated to keep the gluten from developing.

Melt a tablespoon of butter in the frying pan and let cool. In a third bowl, beat ⅓ cup of milk with one egg. Add the cooled butter and pour the mixture into the dry ingredients containing the all-purpose flour. Mix carefully until all the flour is moist, then beat the batter with an electric mixer until it becomes smooth and glossy.

Repeat this step for mixing milk, egg, and shortening. Add this mixture all at once to the dry ingredients containing the cake flour. Stir quickly and lightly until all the flour is moist. You should not have to stir more than 15 seconds. Do not beat the dough and don't worry about any lumps in the batter. How does this batter look compared with the other batter?

Put the batter containing cake flour into four muffin cups. Then put the all-purpose flour batter into the other four cups. Bake for 15 minutes until the tops are brown.

Let the muffins cool. Cut one made with cake flour and one made with all-purpose flour in half.

Observations

Which has the finer grain? Which makes crumbs most easily? Taste the muffins. Which is more tender? Which has large tunnels caused by large bubbles of gas?

Some bread does not contain any protein other than gluten. Why do you think bread dough is kneaded? Why should pie dough be handled lightly?

There are many variations of this experiment. Try making muffins with cake flour and with gluten flour. Handle the batter the same way. See if temperature affects the way gluten develops. Use all-purpose flour but use ice-cold ingredients in one batter and ingredients at room temperature in the other. Which of the following baked products do you think depend on gluten for structure and which must be fairly gluten-free to remain flaky and tender—bread, cream puffs, pie crust, cake, biscuits? Can you think of experiments to test your choices?

6
Kitchen
Chemistry

The first chemists, called alchemists, were not searching for truth about nature or looking for a system to describe all matter. They worked long, hard hours over smelly cauldrons that often contained dangerous materials with a single idea to keep them going—finding a way to create gold.

You can't blame an alchemist for trying. Suppose you had plunged an iron pot into a perfectly ordinary-looking spring and found upon removing the pot some time later that it was covered with a red coating. You might reason, as they did, that if you could turn iron into something else, why not look for a way to make gold? To this end, alchemists separated mixtures and mixed substances together. They developed many procedures used in laboratories today and they discovered many elements no one knew existed.

But the alchemists failed in their intended purpose. No matter how hard they tried, they could not make gold. Perhaps the most important discoveries of the alchemists were events they observed that changed one kind of matter into another, called *chemical reactions.*

There are many different chemical reactions. The flame from a gas burner, the rust on an old piece of iron, and browning of a cut apple exposed to the air are all examples of chemical reactions. Despite differences, all chemical reactions have certain things in common.

Whenever you have a chemical reaction, you start with one kind of matter and end up with another. Often, the products of a reaction have very different properties from the reactants you began with. For example, when propane gas in a stove reacts with oxygen in the air, the products are carbon dioxide and water vapor. This reaction can be written as a chemical equation:

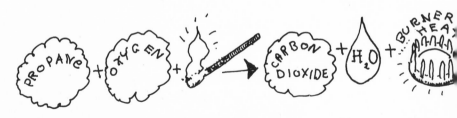

propane gas + oxygen + starter heat ⟶
carbon dioxide + water + burner heat

All chemical reactions involve energy which may be in the form of heat, light, or electricity. Chemists usually find heat is the easiest way to measure energy involved in reactions. There are only two kinds of chemical reactions; ones that give off heat and ones that take up heat. Some reactions, like burning, need heat to get started but give off energy once they get going.

Many times a chemical reaction is not as obvious as the flame of a gas burner. There are many ways of knowing when a chemical reaction has taken place. In this chapter, you will learn some of these ways and how chemical reactions play a part in the preparation of food.

LEMON FIZZ: A REACTION FORMS A GAS

Some reactions form gases as products. When the reaction takes place in a liquid, the bubbles rise to the surface and can be easily observed.

MATERIALS AND EQUIPMENT

baking soda	2 glass tumblers
water	2 spoons
lemonade	

PROCEDURE

Fill one glass half full of water. Stir in ½ teaspoon of baking soda. Does it dissolve easily? Is there any reaction? Use red cabbage indicator (Chapter 2) to test this solution to see if it is an acid or a base.

Fill the second glass half full of lemonade. (Test the lemonade with the indicator.) Use a clean spoon to put ½ teaspoon of baking soda in the lemonade. How can you tell there is a reaction? Drink the lemon fizz quickly before all the bubbles escape into the air.

Observations

Do other experiments to see if baking soda reacts with other acid drinks. Try making orange fizz or apple fizz.

Baking soda is a compound of sodium, carbon, hydrogen, and oxygen. It reacts with acids to give off carbon dioxide.

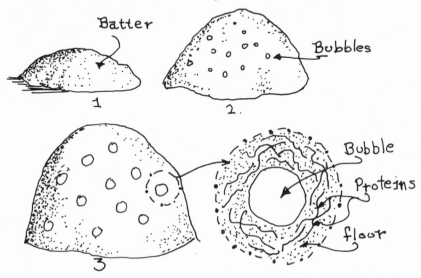

Batter

Bubbles

1

2.

Bubble

Proteins

floor

3

CUPCAKES: HOW CAKES RISE

The changes that occur as a cake bakes are very dramatic. Tiny bubbles of gas form and grow larger as the batter gets warmer. The batter surrounding these bubbles becomes permanently set as the protein from milk and eggs coagulates with heat. Flour strengthens the walls of these bubbles so the cake doesn't collapse when removed from the oven. Sugar and flour hold moisture to make a tender crumb. The ingredients play an important part in the structure of a cake. Perhaps the most remarkable thing about this amazing structure is that it is delicious to eat.

Of course, the structure of a cake would not be possible with-

out a source of bubbles. One source is a chemical reaction like the one in lemon fizz. Before you see how bubbles make a cake rise, do the next experiment to better understand this chemical reaction.

MATERIALS AND EQUIPMENT

(red cabbage indicator)	5 glass tumblers
baking soda	5 spoons
cream of tartar	a candy thermometer
tartaric acid baking powder	a small saucepan
double-acting baking powder	water

PROCEDURE:

Put about ½ teaspoon of cream of tartar in a half a glass of cold water. Stir to dissolve. Is there any reaction? Test a small amount of the solution with red cabbage indicator. Is it acid or base?

Add about ½ teaspoon of baking soda to the cream of tartar solution. Be sure to use a clean spoon for each solution and don't put a wet spoon in the box.

Observations

Is there any reaction? What gas is released? How would your findings from lemon fizz predict this result?

Read the ingredients on the tartaric acid baking-powder container. What ingredients react to produce carbon dioxide? The cornstarch in the baking powder absorbs moisture so that the baking soda and cream of tartar don't react before they are put in a batter. Put ½ teaspoon of this baking powder in ½ glass of cold water. How long does it take for the reaction to start? How long before the reaction is over?

Batter mixed with cream of tartar baking powder must be baked right after it is mixed. If it stands for a while before baking, most of the gas will have escaped and the cake will not rise as well. You can test this by making two batches of cupcakes with cream of tartar baking powder. Let the first batter stand while you mix the second. Bake both batters at the same time. The recipe for cupcakes is given in the next section.

Fill one glass half way with cold water and a second glass half way with hot water. Add ½ teaspoon of double-acting baking powder to each glass. In which glass is the reaction stronger? When no more bubbles are coming out in the first glass, heat the solution in a pan. Is there a second reaction?

Double acting baking powder was developed because it was often inconvenient to have to bake batter as soon as it was mixed. This powder also contains an acid, sodium aluminum sulfate. The acid reacts with baking soda only when heated. Thus carbon dioxide will be produced only when batter is put in the oven.

There were two problems with baking powder containing sodium aluminum sulfate. First, it left a bitter aftertaste in the cake. Secondly, for certain recipes, the heat of the oven might set the structure of the cake before any gas was released, forming a very heavy product. For this reason, double-acting baking powder was developed containing two acid powders. It has quick-acting acid powder, like cream of tartar, that starts releasing carbon dioxide as soon as it is mixed with a liquid. It also contains sodium aluminum sulfate to release more carbon dioxide when it is baked. Less of this acid is needed in such a powder so there is less bitter aftertaste.

PROCEDURE

Heat water until it is about 150°F. (Use the candy thermometer to measure temperature.) Put the hot water in a glass tumbler so that it is half full. Put the candy thermometer in the water. When there is no longer any change in the temperature reading, add a heaping teaspoonful of double-acting baking powder and stir.

Observations

Watch the thermometer as the reaction takes place. Does the solution get warmer or colder? By how many degrees? You can repeat this experiment using different amounts of baking powder.

What you have just witnessed is an example of a chemical reaction that takes up heat. Unlike combustion, where heat is given off, heat must be provided if sodium aluminum sulfate is going to break down and release carbon dioxide. The heat for this reaction is removed from the surrounding liquid, making it cooler.

Use the cupcake recipe given next for experiments to show how different baking powders act in batter. Compare a batch of cupcakes made with cream of tartar baking powder with a batch made with double-acting baking powder. Try making cupcakes with different amounts of baking powder. Use ½ teaspoon for one batch, 1 teaspoon for a second batch, and 1½ teaspoons for a third batch.

If you wish to try one large experiment, first mix a batter with cream of tartar baking powder. Let this batter stand while you mix the rest of the batters. Next mix a batch with double-acting baking powder. Last, mix a batch with cream of tartar baking powder. Bake all three batches together in a muffin tin with twelve cups. Since each batch makes four cupcakes, you can use one muffin tin for the entire experiment. When you compare cupcakes, look for differences in height, crumb size, and taste.

CUPCAKE RECIPE

1 cup cake flour (not self-rising)
½ cup sugar
1 egg
¼ cup butter (½ bar) at room temperature

¼ cup milk
1 teaspoon baking powder
1 teaspoon vanilla extract

Preheat the oven to 350°F. Grease a muffiin tin or put paper baking cups in a muffin tin.

Sift, then measure the flour. Resift with the sugar, salt, and baking powder into a bowl. Set dry ingredients aside.

In a separate bowl soften the butter with an electric mixer. Beat in the egg, milk, and vanilla. Add the liquid ingredients all at one time to the dry ingredients. Stir carefully until all the flour is moistened, then beat just until the batter is smooth. Pour the batter into four muffin cups. Bake for about 15 minutes. The cupcakes are done when the tops are brown and a toothpick stuck into the cupcake comes out clean.

The Rise and Fall

Note: It is fun to watch a cake bake. If you have an oven with a window, leave the light on and look in during the baking process. If you don't have such a window, don't open the oven before it is time for the cupcakes to be done. If a blast of cold air hits a cake before it is finished setting, the hot gas in the cake suddenly contracts and the cake falls. Since the centers set last, a draft often produces a cake with a fallen center.

CARAMEL SYRUP: SUGAR DECOMPOSES

Some compounds, like sugar, break down into simpler compounds and elements when heated. Sugar melts at 320°F and starts to break down or decompose at 356°F. Water is one of the products when sugar breaks down. Carbon is another. As more and more carbon forms, the liquid sugar becomes straw-colored and eventually turns a dark brown. Sugar that has been partly broken down is called *caramel*.

You can see the chemical breakdown of sugar when you make caramel. Be sure to be very careful in following the directions for this experiment because you will be working with very hot material. You should have an adult help you with this experiment.

MATERIALS AND EQUIPMENT

½ cup sugar   a small, heavy frying pan
½ cup water   a wooden spoon

PROCEDURE

Put the sugar in a small, heavy frying pan. Stir continually as you heat the sugar with a medium flame. It will melt and start turning brown. When the sugar is straw-colored, turn off the heat.

Slowly and carefully add ½ cup of water. The caramel will be

brittle and very hot. If you add water too quickly, it may spatter and burn you.

Put a low flame under the pan and stir for another 10 minutes. Try to get all the caramel to dissolve.

When the syrup has cooled, taste it and compare the taste to sugar. Which is sweeter? You can serve this syrup over ice cream or use it to glaze the cupcakes from the last experiment.

If you make caramel again, continue heating the sugar until it is dark brown. Again, turn off the heat and add about ½ cup of water. This time you will have to be even more careful as the caramel is so hot there may be a violent reaction. A solution made dark caramel is used to color gravies and stews. The sugar has been broken down so completely no sweetness remains.

What change in the appearance of the sugar let you know a chemical reaction was taking place? Can you think of any other color changes that are the result of a chemical reaction?

VITAMIN C FRUIT SALAD: OXIDATION OF FRUIT

Certain fruits and vegetables turn brown when a cut surface is exposed to the air. This happens because there is a pigment in fruit that reacts with oxygen in the air. Oxygen is a very reactive element and combines with many substances in a reaction called

"oxidation." Oxidation may be slow, as in the case of the apple, or it may be rapid and produce a flame.

Apples, peaches, pears, and bananas are easily oxidized. A fresh fruit salad, prepared several hours before serving can be protected from oxidation by covering it. The purpose of the following experiment is to see if oxidation can be prevented by treating cut-up fruit with vitamin C.

MATERIALS AND EQUIPMENT

1 apple   a small deep bowl
a peach or ripe pear   2 shallow soup bowls
1 banana   a slotted spoon
1 chewable vitamin C tablet   a sharp knife

PROCEDURE

Put about a cup of water in the small, deep bowl and dissolve the vitamin C tablet in it.

Slice the apple in half. Peel and cut out the core of one half

quickly. Slice this half into the bowl of vitamin C solution. Make sure each slice is covered with the solution. Remove the apple slices with a slotted spoon and put them in one of the shallow bowls.

Peel, core, and slice the other half of the apple directly into the other soup bowl. Repeat this procedure with the other fruit. Slice half into the vitamin C solution and leave slices from the other half untreated. Put all the vitamin C pieces in one bowl and the untreated pieces in the other. Arrange the fruit so that as much surface is exposed to the air as possible, as shown in the illustration.

Let the two fruit salads stand for an hour or more. Watch to see where browning occurs.

Observation

Can you see a difference between the treated and untreated fruit? Why do you think lemon juice is put on apple slices as they are being prepared for apple pie? Do lemons contain vitamin C?

Oxidation of fruit is affected by temperature. You can test this by making two fruit salads. Leave one at room temperature and put the other in the refrigerator. Which salad browns first?

The term "oxidation" is used by chemists for any reaction where substances combine in a manner similar to the way they combine with oxygen. Fruits that oxidize easily will also combine with copper and iron. Put a fruit salad in a copper bowl or an iron pan. Compare browning with a fruit salad in a glass or china bowl. Cover these salads with plastic wrap to reduce oxidation with the air.

All the fruit salads in these experiments are good to eat, even if the fruit is discolored. Combine all the fruit when you have finished experimenting. Add a small can of apricots or some fruit syrup and chill before serving.

FRUIT AND TEA PUNCH: TESTING FOR IRON

What piece of laboratory equipment do you think of first when you read the word "chemistry"? For many nonscientists, the response to that question would be, "test tube." Even a chemist would agree that test tubes are very important to his work because they are designed so that small amounts of material can be put together and the chemist can easily see if there is a chemical reaction.

There are several changes that let you know when a reaction is taking place. In the experiments you have done up to now, you have seen reactions that produce a gas and reactions that produce a color change. Another way is to see a clear solution become cloudy as solid particles form. Such solid particles are called a *precipitate*. You will be looking for a precipitate in the next experiment.

If you have a chemistry set with test tubes, use them for this experiment. If you don't, use small, clear, colorless juice glasses.

There are certain chemicals in tea that react with iron compounds in fruit juices to form a precipitate. This precipitate is very annoying if you are preparing a punch made with tea. Although the punch tastes fine, it does have a muddy look. Since not all fruits contain iron, you can use the following procedure to learn which ones do.

juice glasses or test tubes
about 2 cups of strong tea
an assortment of fruit juices including canned and bottled
juices, red juices, pineapple juice, and prune juice.

PROCEDURE

Set out a row of small glasses or test tubes and put about an inch of tea in each glass. Label the glasses for each juice you are going to test. You might also want to prepare a data sheet to record your observations. Here is an example of what a data sheet might look like:

FRUIT JUICE	TEST RESULT
orange	−
canned pineapple	+
cranberry	?
cherry Hi-C	?

Add about an inch of juice to each glass of tea. Watch for cloudiness. If a precipitate forms put a + mark next to the name of the juice on your data sheet. If no precipitate forms and the mixture remains clear, put a − sign. If you are not certain put a

? on the data sheet and test the juice again. Some juices are cloudy to begin with. Make sure that a new precipitate forms by comparing the tea mixture with a plain sample of juice.

What juices contain iron? Do canned juices contain more iron than bottled juices? According to a table of food composition, the juices that contain the most iron are red juices, pineapple, and prune juice. Do your findings agree with this?

When you have finished the experiment, pour all the mixtures into a pitcher. Taste it to see if you might like to add more of any particular juice. Add any leftover tea. Pour over ice to serve.

7
Plants We Eat

All living things need a constant supply of energy in order to stay alive. The energy comes from a great number of chemical reactions where food combines with oxygen. When sugar, for example, reacts with oxygen, the end products are carbon dioxide, water, and energy. The reaction can be written:

sugar + oxygen ──────→ carbon dioxide + water + energy

Scientists have measured the amounts of energy given off when different kinds of food combine with oxygen. They put weighed amounts of food in a special instrument called a *calorimeter*. The food is burned with oxygen and the heat energy given off by the reaction raises the temperature of the water outside the chamber where the food is burning. The change in temperature of the water is a measure of the amount of energy in the food. This heat is measured in *calories*. If you look in most general cookbooks, you can find a table that states the calories in different foods. Fats have the most calories and proteins have the least.

We use energy we get from food for moving and thinking and responding to the world. In addition, a great deal of energy from food goes for building new molecules of protein and carbohydrates in our bodies. Any leftover energy not used for these activities is used to build fat molecules. The average growing boy or girl needs between 2600 and 3000 calories a day. If you eat more than this and don't do enough to use them up, you will gain weight.

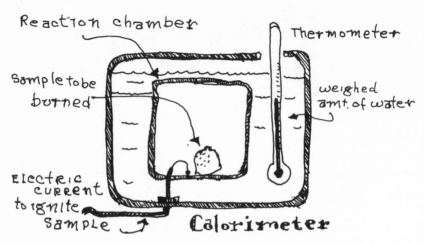

Energy in food is passed from one living thing to another. As one organism feeds on another, a food chain is formed. The question is, Where does the food chain end? The living things at the end of the food chain must be able to get energy from some source other than feeding on other living things and must be able to convert this energy into a substance that is food. On our planet, the end of the food chain is green plants.

The reaction that forms food in green plants is the reverse of the reaction in our bodies when we oxidize sugar:

carbon dioxide + water + energy ⟶ sugar + oxygen

The outside source of energy for this reaction is sunlight. The green pigment *chlorophyll* is most directly responsible for the ability of plants to make sugar. This process of food manufacturing is called *photosynthesis* which means "putting together with light."

Plants use sugar made during photosynthesis to make proteins and carbohydrates.

When animals eat plants they get energy that originally came from the sun. The importance of green plants to all other forms of life on earth is clear. Without them, we would not survive.

The experiments in this chapter will show you some of the activities of plants that help keep them alive so that other forms of life may always have food.

RAW VEGETABLE SALAD: HOW PLANTS TAKE IN WATER

The roots of a plant have many jobs. Most roots anchor a plant to the ground. Some roots, like a carrot, store food made in leaves. But the most important job is to absorb water from the soil.

Look at the tip of a fresh carrot that has not been trimmed or packaged. The main root becomes very slender at the tip and there are many small roots sticking out from it. Look at these smaller roots with a magnifying glass. There are many tiny branches of each rootlet which increases the surface area of the root so more water can be absorbed. (Note: If you can't get an untrimmed carrot, put a fresh carrot, tip down, in a glass of water. It will develop new roots in a few days.)

Water is absorbed into roots by a process called *osmosis*. In osmosis, water passes through a thin sheet of living material called a *cell membrane*. Cell membranes have holes in them that are larger than water molecules.

Since the holes in cell membranes are larger than water molecules, you might wonder why water flows *into* roots when it could just as easily flow out. The next experiment will give you an answer.

MATERIALS AND EQUIPMENT

a large carrot	a vegetable parer
salt	2 bowls
water	2 spoons

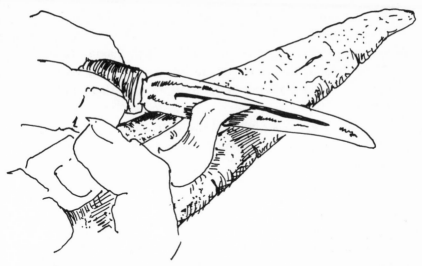

PROCEDURE

Peel the carrot with the parer. (Be sure to move the parer away from your fingers.) Use the parer to make strips of carrot.

Divide the parings into two groups and put a group in each bowl. Add enough fresh water to each bowl to completely cover the parings. Put about a tablespoon of salt into one of the bowls and stir. The water should taste very salty.

Let the parings soak for several hours. From time to time, take out a paring from each dish and bend it and taste it to see how crisp it is.

Observations

Which parings are crisper? Which parings have absorbed water and which have lost water?

You can do many variations of this experiment with other vegetables. Thin slices of cucumber are especially good. Try different amounts of salt to see how fast wilting occurs. Find out if wilting occurs more quickly in warm (not hot) water than in cold water.

The direction water flows in roots depends on the minerals dissolved in the water. When more minerals are inside the roots than in soil water, water flows into the roots, making them firm and crisp. When there are more minerals in the soil water than in root cells water flows *out* of the roots, making them wilted and soft.

You can make a salad with all the vegetables from this experiment. Chill, then drain, the vegetables. Make a dressing of sour cream and fresh chopped dill or parsley to serve.

STRIPED CELERY SNACK: HOW WATER MOVES UP STEMS

One of the important jobs of stems is to carry water from the roots to the leaves. You can see how this happens if you put a stalk of celery in half a glass of water colored with about a teaspoon of red food coloring.

When the water has moved all the way up the stem, use a vegetable parer to shave away the outer surface of the celery. Which parts of the stem have the most food coloring? The long strands that carry water are called the *xylem*. Xylem is made of hollow cells that form a pipeline from roots to leaves. You can see where the xylem is in celery by cutting across the stalk.

Repeat this experiment, using two stalks of celery. One stalk should be quite leafy and the other should have no leaves.

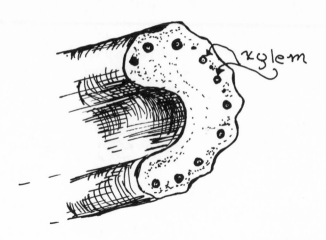

xylem

Observations

In which stalk does the water reach the top of the stem first?

Do another experiment with two leafy stalks of celery. Put one in the sunlight and put a small plastic bag over the other. In which stalk does the water rise more quickly? How do your findings support the theory that the speed with which water rises in plants is a result of how fast water evaporates from the leaves?

You can eat the celery when you have finished your experiments. Cut the celery into two-inch lengths and sprinkle with garlic salt and paprika.

Try putting other vegetables in colored water. See if you can find the xylem in white radishes, scallions, and carrots. Choose a vegetable dye that will show up against the color of the vegetables.

SPINACH: COLOR CHANGES IN CHLOROPHYLL

"Eat your spinach," has been said by so many mothers that you can't help wondering why so many children dislike this vegetable. It is especially curious as many of the greatest chefs in the world have created dishes based on spinach that are considered a rare treat by food lovers. Perhaps one reason children don't like spinach is that it is not often prepared properly. All too often, cooked spinach is a limp, unappetizing gray-green.

Fresh spinach, on the other hand, is a beautiful, rich green. When it is first put in boiling water, this green brightens as gases in the cells are forced out by heating. After this, the spinach becomes grayer and grayer. Cooking releases certain acids in spinach which change the color of chlorophyll.

The amount of acid that is released during cooking is very small. It would be possible to keep spinach a bright green if this acid could be removed as soon as it forms. A pinch of baking soda, added to the cooking water, will react with the acid and "neutralize" it. (You can try this to see if it does in fact happen.) Baking soda, however, makes vegetables mushy, so it is not often used. (More about this in the next experiment.)

When chemists want to prevent a solution from becoming too acid or basic, they use another kind of solution called a buffer. Buffers can absorb any acid or basic molecules and take them out of solution as they are released into solution. Of course, many buffers used in laboratories are not suitable for eating. But one substance we do eat that can act as a buffer is milk.

It should be possible to preserve the color of spinach by cooking it in milk. Do the next experiment to find out.

MATERIALS AND EQUIPMENT

fresh, washed spinach   a slotted spoon
milk   2 saucepans
water   a measuring cup
                             a white plate

PROCEDURE

Put a cup of milk in one saucepan and a cup of water in the other. Heat the liquids on a low flame. When they begin to simmer, drop a few leaves of spinach into each pan. Keep the temperature low so that the milk simmers but doesn't boil. Cook for 4 or 5 minutes. Turn off the heat and let the spinach stay in the hot liquids for another few minutes.

Remove the spinach with a slotted spoon to a white plate so you can compare the colors of the cooked spinach with that of the raw spinach. Have the colors changed due to cooking? Which spinach seems grayer, the spinach cooked in water or the spinach cooked in milk?

Choose either milk or water to cook the rest of the spinach. Season with salt, pepper, and butter to serve.

The experiment you did to show how water gets into plants also showed how water is important for support. Without water, plants become wilted and limp. But in addition to water, plants contain a carbohydrate, called *cellulose,* that plays an important role in the supporting structure of a plant.

The soft protoplasm of each plant cell is surrounded on all sides by a cell wall made up mainly of cellulose. Cellulose is firmer than protoplasm and the cell walls help to support a plant against the force of gravity.

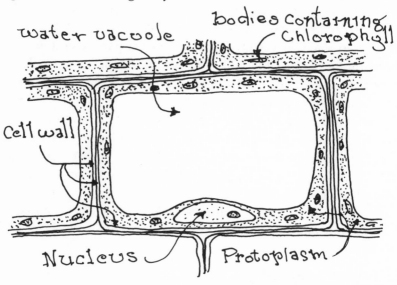

Like starches, cellulose is made of chains of sugar molecules linked together. It would be a good source of food for us if we could digest it but, unfortunately, we can't. The sugar molecules in cellulose are linked together differently than the linkages in starch. Cellulose links make the chain rigid and make it useless to us as food because we have no way of breaking these links in our digestive tracts. Some animals, like cows, have microorganisms in their stomachs that can break down the links in a cellulose chain. They can live on hay and grass. But the cellulose in plants we eat leaves our bodies pretty much as it entered.

The main reason we cook vegetables is to soften the cellulose so that it passes through our bodies more easily. The next experiment shows some of the conditions that change the rate at which cellulose softens.

MATERIALS AND EQUIPMENT

a small butternut or other hard   a vegetable parer
   winter squash   a sharp knife and cutting
vinegar   board
baking soda   measuring spoons
   a slotted spoon
   3 saucepans

PROCEDURE

Peel the squash with the vegetable parer. Cut the squash in half. (Be careful, it may be hard to cut.) Scrape out the seeds and pith with a spoon. Cut the squash into one-inch cubes, trying to keep them as much alike as possible.

Divide the squash into three saucepans and cover each with water. Add a teaspoon of vinegar to one pan and ½ teaspoon of baking soda to another. Leave the third pan with plain water, as a control.

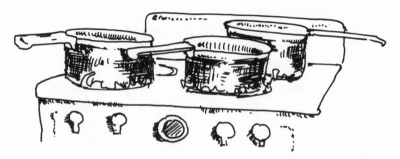

Light the burner under each pan, keeping the flame the same size. Bring each pan to a boil and let it continue boiling while you make your observations.

Every few minutes remove a piece of squash from each pan with a slotted spoon. Test it for softness by trying to mash it with a fork.

Observations

Which squash becomes soft first? Does cooking squash in acid speed up the rate of softening cellulose?

When all the squash is cooked, drain it and season with butter, salt, and pepper to serve.

As you might expect, the length of cooking time for vegetables depends on the amount of cellulose in the plant. Leafy vegetables, such as spinach, do not contain much cellulose and need only be cooked a few minutes. Artichokes, on the other hand, are high in cellulose and must be cooked quite awhile to get soft. Design an experiment to check this idea out.

CHOP SUEY: HOW BEANS SPROUT

The chief source of food for most of the people of the world is seeds. Cereal grains, corn, rice, and beans are all seeds. The food seeds contain is there for a good reason—to nourish a baby plant until leaves develop and it can make its own food.

Every seed is a remarkable package. It appears to be very simple. Yet it contains the cells that will become a plant and all the food needed for the baby plant to get a good start. Seeds are able to go through long periods of dryness and extreme cold, only to burst with new life when conditions are right.

You can create the right conditions for sprouting seeds in your kitchen. Sprouts are also an especially delicious vegetable, as many cooks will tell you.

MATERIALS AND EQUIPMENT

¼ cup dried beans such as lentils, limas, kidneys, and blackeyes

water
a clean, unglazed pot (a new flowerpot is good)
a saucer to cover the pot
a bowl
a colander

PROCEDURE

Put the beans in the bowl and cover with water. Let them soak overnight. The starch in the beans absorbs the water and the beans will swell.

The next day, moisten the inside of a new flowerpot with water. Drain the beans in a colander and put them in the flowerpot. In order for beans to sprout, they must be kept moist but not wet. Cover the pot with the saucer and put it in a closet.

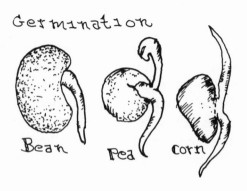

Germination

Bean   Pea   Corn

Check the beans every day. If they appear dry or develop the smell of fermenting beans, wash them by running water over them in a colander and drain them well. Rinse out the pot before you return the beans to it.

The first structure to grow from a seed is the root. This anchors the seedling to the ground and makes sure that there will be a continuous supply of water for the growing plant. Beans have two seedling leaves that contain stored food. (Do these contain chlorophyll when they first emerge?) When beans sprout in soil, these thick leaves are pushed up through the soil and become green. They make food until the thinner, foliage leaves develop, when they shrivel and die.

Observations

There are many experiments you can do to see how different conditions affect the sprouting of seeds. Put some soaked seeds in the refrigerator and compare them with seeds sprouting at room temperature. Find out if light and darkness affect sprouting. Take a few seeds just when the roots appear and put them between two pieces of moist blotting paper held together by paper clips. Keep the blotting paper moist and prop it so the roots are pointed upwards, away from the pull of gravity. Watch to see how these roots grow after several days.

Add the sprouts to canned or frozen chop suey and heat just until hot. They should be crisp to eat.

POPCORN: MEASURING WATER IN SEEDS

No matter how dry seeds seem to be, all seeds contain a tiny bit of water that keeps the cells alive until conditions are favorable for sprouting. It is this tiny bit of water that makes popcorn possible.

When a kernel of popping corn is heated quickly, the water inside the kernel becomes a gas that exerts pressure strong enough to burst the tough seed coat. Once free of its container, the gas expands rapidly, causing the softer material inside the seed to puff up.

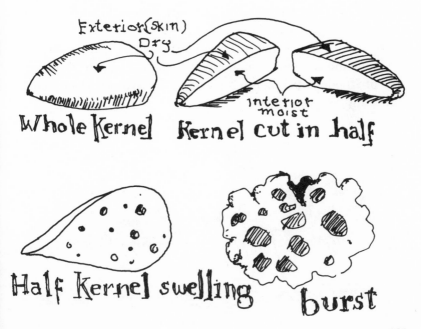

Exterior (skin) Dry

interior moist

Whole Kernel   Kernel cut in half

Half Kernel swelling   burst

You might guess that the way corn pops depends on the amount of moisture in the seed. This is what the next experiment is designed to find out.

MATERIALS AND EQUIPMENT

fresh popping corn	a measuring cup
a shallow pan	a 6-inch ruler
a pot with a cover	pencil and paper

PROCEDURE

Preheat the oven to 200°F. Count the number of kernels in ¼ cup of fresh popping corn. Spread the corn in a single layer in a shallow pan and put it in the oven for an hour and a half.

Count out an equal number of kernels of fresh popping corn. Put about 3 tablespoons of oil in the bottom of a pot, just enough to cover it. Heat the oil over a high flame until it starts to smoke. Add the fresh popping corn. The kernels should make a single layer on the bottom of the pan. Cover and shake over a lower flame until popping stops. Remove the popcorn from the heat.

Count the number of unpopped kernels. Measure the longest side of 20 popped kernels with a ruler. Write down all of your figures and average them.

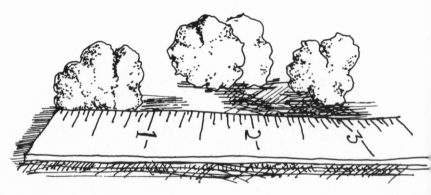

At the end of an hour and a half, remove the popping corn from the oven. (Did any kernels pop when heated slowly?) When they have cooled, pop these kernels the same way you popped the first batch. Count the number of unpopped kernels and measure 20 of these popped kernels.

Observations

How does the average size of the heated corn compare to the average size of the fresh popping corn? What do you think heating in the oven did to the corn?

You can do many variations on this experiment. Take ¼ cup of kernels and put them in a dish exposed to the air for several weeks. Compare popcorn made with these kernels to that of fresh popping corn. Add water to popping corn by putting a small amount of water in a jar, just enough to coat each kernel when the jar is shaken. Keep the jar covered. After several days, pop this corn. You might also compare popcorn that has been heated in a slow oven for different amounts of time. See how long it has to be heated before most of the corn will not pop.

8
Microbes

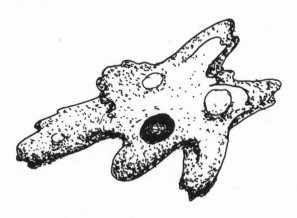

One of the first things man must have learned about food was that it often changed in an unpleasant way if it was allowed to stand. Many kinds of food develop a foul odor and become mushy. Such food is not only unappetizing, it can make you ill.

Cooking probably began as a way of delaying spoilage. People also learned to use strong spices and herbs to mask the flavor of food that was no longer fresh. It is not surprising that the strongest spices like pepper, chili, and curry were first used in hot climates, where food spoils more quickly, rather than in colder parts of the world.

But not all the changes in food left to stand were unpleasant. Sometimes milk became cheese, grape juice became wine, flour and water paste developed bubbles and became bread when baked. These pleasant changes became a way of preserving food. Cheese and wine could be eaten months after they were prepared. Stored grain could be made into flour at some later time.

In days when there were no such things as canning, freezing, or refrigerating food, cheese, bread, and wine were a protection against famine—a time when there was no fresh food. No wonder they were among the most important foods of early civilizations.

The change in grape juice as it became wine was so well known that it had its own name, *fermentation,* meaning "to boil." As grape juice ferments, tiny bubbles form that are similar to bubbles in boiling liquids, except that the grape juice is not hot. We began to understand what was going on in all these food changes when something went wrong with the wine industry in France.

The grape juice still fermented but the product had a terrible taste. Since the spoiled wine was prepared in exactly the same way as wine that was good, the winemakers couldn't understand how spoiling could occur. In desperation, they called in a great scientist, Louis Pasteur, to solve their problem.

Pasteur studied the wine in good vats and in spoiled vats. He found that both fermentation and wine spoilage were products of living things that could only be seen with a microscope. The microbe that fermented grape juice to wine used sugar from grapes as food and produced alcohol and carbon dioxide as waste products. The microbes that spoiled the wine used alcohol formed by the first microbes as food. It was the wastes of these second microbes that gave the wine a bad taste.

The solution of the winemakers' problem was simple. Kill the microbes by heating the wine gently to denature the protein in the microbes. This heating process, called pasteurization, is a standard procedure today for killing harmful microbes in dairy products, beer, and wine.

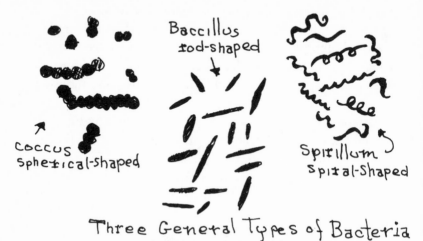

Three General Types of Bacteria

Microbes are everywhere, in air, in water, in the soil, in our bodies. The study of microbes has touched on all aspects of human life including agriculture, medicine, chemical products for industry, and food preparation and preservation.

The experiments in this chapter will show you how we use microbes for some foods we eat.

SALLY LUNN BREAD: A STUDY OF YEAST ACTIVITY

Yeasts are one-celled plants that are distant cousins of mushrooms. Like mushrooms and other plants that do not contain chlorophyll, yeast plants cannot make their own food and must get it from their surroundings. When conditions are not favorable, yeasts become inactive, only to spring to life when conditions are right.

The life cycle of brewers' yeast

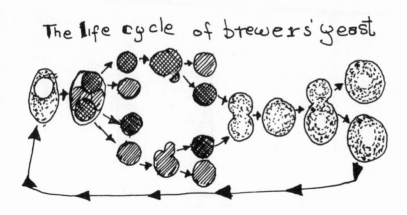

The products of fermentation, alcohol and carbon dioxide, are of great importance to the winemaker and baker. The winemaker is interested in alcohol production and the baker is interested in carbon dioxide, for it is this gas that makes his bread rise.

The purpose of the next experiment is to see what food yeasts need for growth. Other conditions for growth, temperature and moisture, will be made as favorable as possible.

MATERIALS AND EQUIPMENT

sugar	a measuring cup
corn syrup	a candy thermometer
cornstarch	3 six-ounce glasses
water	a large pot
a package of dry yeast	3 spoons
	measuring spoons

PROCEDURE

Dissolve the yeast in ½ cup of 90°F water. Divide the yeast mixture equally in three small glasses. Set up a warm water bath for the yeast in the large pot. Put enough 90°F water in the pot so that the glasses containing the yeast mixture sit in the water without it spilling into the glasses, as in the illustration on p. 108.

Put 1 tablespoon of sugar in the first glass, 1 tablespoon of corn syrup in the next glass, and 1 tablespoon of cornstarch in the third glass. Stir each glass with a different spoon.

Put all three glasses in the warm water bath. Measure fermentation by the size of the bubbles in the foam and the rate at which they form.

Observations

The material a microbe uses as food is called a *substrate*. Which substrate in your experiment starts being fermented first? Which substrate has the steadiest rate of fermentation? Can you smell the alcohol produced by fermentation?

Glucose is the principle food of yeast used for baking. When yeast comes in contact with glucose, fermentation begins immediately. Glucose is present in corn syrup. Yeast can also get glucose from sucrose (table sugar) and starch but it takes longer to get going, as sucrose and starch have to be broken down into simpler sugars before fermentation can occur. How do your findings support this idea?

You can use your experiment to see how fermenting yeast makes bread rise.

all the mixtures from your experiment
about 3½ cups all-purpose
flour

1 teaspoon salt
½ cup milk
1 bar butter
3 eggs

PROCEDURE

Put the milk and butter in a saucepan and heat until the milk is about 85°F. Don't let the milk get too hot or you will kill the yeast. Pour all three glasses of your experiment into a large bowl and add the milk and butter mixture.

Add about a cup of the flour and the salt to the liquids. Mix at a low speed with an electric mixer. When all the flour is moistened, beat the batter for about two minutes at a medium speed to develop the gluten. Beat in the eggs and add another cup of flour. Finally add enough of the remaining flour to make a stiff batter that can still be stirred.

Cover the bowl with a moist, clean dish towel and place in a warm spot to rise, such as the pot storage cabinet next to a warm oven or on top of the pilot light of your stove. Let the batter rise until it is double in size—about an hour.

While the batter is rising, grease an 8″ × 4″ loaf pan and sprinkle a few tablespoons of flour on the pan. Shake it so that the grease is evenly coated and dump out any extra flour.

Push the batter down. What gives the batter its stretchy consistency? Examine the air pockets in the batter. Are they evenly distributed? Are there larger air pockets near the source of heat? Beat the batter for about 30 seconds. Put the batter in the loaf pan, cover with the dish towel and let the batter rise again until it is double in size. Preheat the oven to 325°F.

Bake the bread at 325°F for about 50 minutes. It is done when the sides draw slightly away from the sides of the pan. Run a sharp knife around the bread as soon as you take it from the oven. Remove the bread and let it cool on a wire rack. Sally Lunn bread is best served while still warm.

Observations

You can do many experiments to see how different conditions affect fermentation. Try putting the same amounts of yeast, water, and sugar in different temperatures. See how different amounts of sugar affect fermentation. You can use your experiments in many baked products.

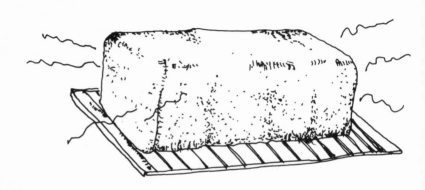

PRETZELS: INHIBITING YEAST ACTION

The addition of other chemicals to the yeast environment can have an effect on fermentation. The next experiment shows how.

MATERIALS AND EQUIPMENT

sugar

salt

1 cake active yeast, fresh

3 spoons

a measuring cup

a candy thermometer

3 juice glasses

a large pot

Dissolve the yeast in 1 cup of 85°F water. Divide the yeast solution into three juice glasses.

Put ¼ teaspoon sugar in the first glass and ¼ teaspoon salt and ¼ teaspoon sugar in the second glass. Leave the third glass untreated as a control. Stir each glass with a different spoon.

Make a warm water bath in a pot as you did for the previous experiment. Put the three glasses in the water bath and watch for fermentation activity.

Observations

Which glass has the most activity? Which glass has the least? Does salt inhibit yeast activity? How can you tell?

Use this experiment to make pretzels.

MATERIALS AND EQUIPMENT

contents of juice glasses from your experiment
about 4½ cups all-purpose flour
an egg yolk beaten with about 1 tablespoon water
coarse (kosher) salt

Pour the contents of your experiment into a large bowl. Add between 4 and 4½ cups flour. Mix to form a stiff dough.

Knead the dough on a floured surface for about eight minutes. Kneading develops the gluten which is the only protein that supports pretzels. (Sally Lunn bread has milk and eggs to help do this job.) To knead, fold the side of the dough farthest from you over, toward you. Push the fold into the rest of the dough with the heel of your hand. Give the dough a quarter turn and repeat the motion. Dough that has been properly kneaded is no longer sticky but smooth and elastic.

Oil a large bowl and put in the kneaded dough, turning it so the surface becomes slightly oiled and will not dry out. Cover the dough with a clean, damp towel. Let it rise in a warm place until double in size.

Punch down the dough with your fist. Grease a cookie sheet. Shape the dough into pretzels and put them on the sheet. You can make many different shapes.

Use a pastry brush to paint each pretzel with egg yolk that has been beaten with a tablespoon of water. Sprinkle the pretzels with coarse salt.

Preheat the oven to 475°F. Let the pretzels rise again in a warm place until they are almost double in size. Bake for about 10 minutes or until the pretzels are firm and golden brown.

YOGURT: HOW BACTERIA PRODUCE LACTIC ACID

Bacteria are one-celled microbes that are smaller than yeast. Bacteria, like yeast, must also get food from their surroundings. Bacteria can use many substances as food. Some even live on such unappetizing materials as rubber and petroleum. The bacteria you will be experimenting with live on milk.

Milk is a mixture of many kinds of substances. One of these is lactose, a sugar found only in milk. Certain bacteria feed on lactose and give off *lactic acid* as a waste product.

As lactic acid bacteria grow, more and more lactic acid collects, giving the milk a sour taste, typical of acids. What is even more striking than the change in taste is the change in texture. Lactic acid causes milk proteins to become denatured, making the milk become thicker and thicker. Such cultured milk, called yogurt, has a nutty, sour taste and a custardy texture.

It is simple to make yogurt at home. The recipe, which follows, is certain to produce good results because you will be creating ideal conditions for the growth of lactic acid bacteria. Use the recipe as a starting point to learn about these microbes. Try making yogurt at different temperatures. Compare yogurt made with fresh whole milk, condensed milk, and powdered milk. Find out

what happens when you add sugar to the milk. Use different brands of commercially prepared yogurt as a starter culture. See how many generations of yogurt you can produce from the yogurt you make. Use red cabbage indicator to measure changes in acidity as the culture grows.

MATERIALS AND EQUIPMENT

1 container of commercially prepared plain yogurt

1 quart skim milk (powdered dry milk can be used)

a measuring cup

a candy thermometer

a saucepan

a clean glass container that will hold 1 quart of liquid

a towel

PROCEDURE

Warm the milk in the pan until a skin rises (160°F). This kills any bacteria that may cause the milk to spoil before the yogurt forms. Cool the milk until it is 110°F.

Take about ½ container of yogurt and add an equal amount of warm milk to it. When this is thoroughly mixed, add the rest of the yogurt and stir. This is your "starter" culture.

Gently stir the starter into the rest of the milk in the pan.

Pour the entire mixture into the glass container. Wrap a towel around it to keep in the heat. Let the yogurt culture stand, undisturbed, covered or uncovered at room temperature for 8–12 hours. The yogurt is finished when it moves away from the side of the container in one piece if you tilt it.

Refrigerate the finished yogurt to stop the growth of the bacteria. Homemade yogurt is not quite as thick as commercially prepared yogurt.

Yogurt may be eaten plain or mixed with fruit preserves, honey, maple syrup, or a small amount of defrosted, concentrated orange juice.

9
Enzymes

In 1897 Eduard Büchner, a German chemist, ground up some yeast cells and made an extract from them. He put this extract in grape juice and found, to his astonishment, that the grape juice still fermented. For the first time, glucose became alcohol and carbon dioxide without using living cells. The substance in Büchner's extract that caused fermentation was called "enzyme" meaning "in yeast."

Today we think of enzymes as the molecules that control the countless numbers of chemical reactions in living organisms. This may not seem like an important job until you take a close look at some of the reactions that take place in a living thing. The oxidation of food, for example, does not burn in your body the way it burns in a calorimeter. If it did, a piece of chocolate cake containing 400 calories would raise the body temperature of a 100-pound person to about 117°F, high enough to cause death. In your body, food combines with many different substances in a chain of reactions where a little energy is released with each step. Controlled release of energy permits it to be used for the work that must be done in the body. And it is enzymes controlling all these reactions that make life possible.

A few enzymes are prepared commercially for use in food making. You can use them to begin your own investigation of enzyme action.

JUNKET: A STUDY OF ENZYME ACTION

One of the first steps in the digestion of milk is denaturing milk protein so it becomes more solid. If milk remained a liquid, it would quickly pass through the stomach before it could be digested. But denatured milk moves slowly enough for digestion to take place.

A great many things will denature milk protein, including heat and acids. In the stomach of mammals, milk protein is denatured by an enzyme called *rennin* (or sometimes, rennet).

Rennin is commercially prepared from the linings of calves' stomachs. Rennin tablets are used to prepare cottage cheese and thicken milk desserts. The next experiment will show you some of the properties of enzymes by showing you the conditions necessary for rennin to work. Since rennin tablets are hard to buy, you will be experimenting with Junket, a custardlike milk dessert that contains the enzyme.

milk

1 box Junket (any flavor)

3 bowls

a saucepan

measuring spoons

candy thermometer

a spoon

a measuring cup

Put two tablespoons of Junket in each bowl. Heat ⅔ cup of milk to about 160°F. Mix this hot milk into one of the bowls of Junket.

Heat another ⅔ cup of milk to 110°F and stir into another bowl of Junket. Mix ⅔ cup of cold milk into the third dish of Junket.

Observations

In which dish does the Junket become firm most quickly? In which dish does the Junket fail to set? How does this support the idea that enzymes are proteins? *Hint:* What happens to proteins when they are heated to a high temperature?

Do an experiment to see if Junket will work on other proteins. Make Junket with soybean milk or coconut milk. (You can get soybean milk at health food stores and many general cookbooks will tell you how to prepare coconut milk.) Suppose you denature milk some other way, like boiling milk. Let the boiled milk cool to 110°F before adding the Junket. Does the Junket set? How do your findings support the idea that rennin, like many other enzymes, controls only one reaction—in this case, denaturing milk protein?

Papaya melons

BAKED STEAK: ACIDS, BASES, AND ENZYME ACTION

Papain is an enzyme that is commercially prepared from a tropical melon. It is one of a number of enzymes found in plants and animals that break down proteins. For this reason, papain is sold as a meat tenderizer.

The purpose of the next experiment is to answer two questions: Is meat treated with papain more tender than untreated meat? Does an acid or a base have an effect on the tenderizing activity of papain?

The biggest problem in this experiment is in measuring the tenderness of meat. In a laboratory, you could measure tenderness with all kinds of complicated procedures. But in a kitchen, where you don't have elaborate equipment, you have to use another kind of measurement. After trying several techniques, like cutting the meat with a knife or piercing it with a fork, we found the best method was to count the total number of chews before each piece was swallowed.

Needless to say, counting chews is not the most precise method of measuring tenderness. Two pieces of meat, prepared in exactly the same manner, might require different numbers of chews depending on the size of the pieces, whether or not there was gristle, how it tasted, how dry the chewer's mouth was, and whether or not the chewer expected it to be tender.

Since there are so many known possibilities of error, the procedure for this experiment is the most elaborate one in this book.

You will be taking precautions wherever possible to reduce the sources of error.

MATERIALS AND EQUIPMENT

3/4 pound round steak. (When you buy the steak, look for the most homogeneous piece with very little fat and gristle and a uniform thickness.)

unseasoned meat tenderizer
vinegar
baking soda
water

measuring spoons
a fork
6 shallow dessert dishes
6 spoons
5 juice glasses
a broiling pan
a cutting board
a sharp knife
a pot with a cover
index cards
scissors
pencil and paper
6 paper plates

a hungry friend who doesn't know anything about your experiment. Tell your friend you will call when you are ready.

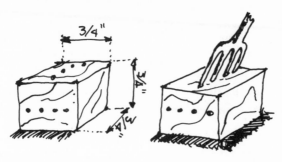

Trim any fat and gristle from the meat and cut the trimmed meat into ¾ inch cubes. Try to keep the size of the cubes as uniform as possible. Pierce each piece of meat twice with a fork. (This is to allow the solutions you will be putting on the meat to penetrate inside.) Mix up all the cubes of meat in a pile.

Set out in a row the six shallow dishes. Deal out the cubes of meat, as you would deal cards, into the six dishes to form six equal groups of meat cubes. Try and get the same number in each group. If you have any extra pieces put them in the last (control) group. Number the groups 1 through 6 going from left to right.

Put juice glasses in front of groups 1 through 5 and put two tablespoons of water in each glass. Put two tablespoons of water on the meat in group 6.

Put ¼ teaspoon of meat tenderizer in the glasses in front of groups 1, 2, and 4.

Put ½ teaspoon of vinegar in the solutions for groups 2 and 3. Put ½ teaspoon baking soda into the glasses for groups 4 and 5. The solution for each group is:

> Group 1 Meat tenderizer and water
> Group 2 Meat tenderizer, acid, water
> Group 3 Acid, water
> Group 4 Meat tenderizer, base, water
> Group 5 Base, water
> Group 6 Water

Stir each solution with a different spoon and pour over each group of meat cubes. Use the spoons to thoroughly moisten the meat in each group.

Preheat the oven to 400°F. Let the meat stand in the solutions while you complete this step.

The order in which each piece of meat is chewed can affect your results. The best way to reduce this source of error is to present each piece of meat in an order determined by chance. To do this, you have to prepare a table of numbers for each piece of meat that has a random order. Here's how to do it:

1   Cut the index cards into as many small squares as the *total number* of pieces of meat in your experiment. If you have 6 groups of 10 pieces each, you will need 60 small squares.

2   Put the numeral "1" on as many squares of card as you have pieces of meat in group 1. If you have 10 pieces, 10 squares of index card should be marked "1." Do the same for groups 2,3,4,5, and 6.

3   Put all the marked squares of card in a pot. Cover the pot and shake it to mix up all the squares. Draw out one square at a time, without looking, and mark down the numeral on a piece of paper. The order might look something like this:

4,4,6,6,6,2,1,1,3,5,6,4, . . . etc.

When you have made out your table of random numbers, go on to drain the solutions from each dish and put the drained meat on the broiling pan in separate groups. Keep the groups in the right order so you know which is which. Arrange the meat so that all the pieces will be heated the same. Bake for 15 minutes.

Observations

While the meat is baking, prepare a sheet of paper to record your data:

NUMBER OF CHEWS

Group 1	Group 2	Group 3	Group 4	Group 5	Group 6

Test the meat for doneness by pressing with a fork. It should be springy and firm. Meat that is rare will be softer as all the protein has not been set by heat.

Number the paper plates 1 through 6 and put each group of cubes on the proper plate. Set up a table with some kind of barrier so your friend cannot see where each piece comes from. Get your data sheet and pencil, your table of random numbers and call your friend.

Collecting the Data

Show your friend where to sit. Tell him that you are going to give him pieces of meat to eat and that you are testing the meat for tenderness. Ask him to count the number of chews needed before he swallows the meat. Tell him to chew as naturally as possible.

Your table of random numbers tells you the order for choosing each piece of meat. If the first three numerals were 4,4,6 . . . you would give your friend a piece from Group 4, another piece from Group 4, and a piece from Group 6, in that order. Check off each number on your table as your friend chews the meat.

Observations

Record the number of chews for each piece in the proper column on your data sheet. When you have the data for all the pieces of meat, take the average for each group. Was meat treated with tenderizer more tender than untreated meat? (Compare the averages for Group 1 with Group 6.) Did acid or base alone affect meat tenderness? (Compare Groups 3 and 5 with

Group 6.) Did acid have an effect on the action of the enzyme? (Compare Groups 1 and 2.) Did a base have an effect on enzyme action? Compare Groups 1 and 4.)

If you are not certain of your results, compare them with the data on the next page that I obtained when I did the experiment. Your numbers may be very different but you probably will come to the same conclusions.

You can use the procedure for this experiment to do many other experiments. See if you get similar results with another acid, such as vitamin C. Try the experiment on other kinds of meat. Find out if the enzyme has any other effect on meat, like juiciness. Can you think of a way to modify the procedure so you can measure juiciness? You might find using another kind of meat, like hamburger, useful for studying the enzyme's effect on juiciness. You might also do experiments to see if you can denature the enzyme by heating it. Boil an enzyme solution before you put it on the meat and compare its activity with an unheated enzyme solution.

DATA FOR NUMBER OF CHEWS

	Group 1	Group 2	Group 3	Group 4	Group 5	Group 6
	26	42	54	25	44	45
	35	33	53	28	22	29
	29	25	48	20	27	54
	32	35	30	18	47	37
						60
Average	30.5	33.8	46.2	22.8	35.0	45.0

Note: The data show a great deal of variability. The experiment should be repeated several times to make certain of the results. If your data differ it may mean that you are right and that these data are incorrect.

About the Author

Vicki Cobb was born in New York City and received her early education at the Little Red Schoolhouse. She attended the University of Wisconsin on a Ford Foundation Early Admissions Scholarship, and in 1958 received her bachelor's degree from Barnard College. She earned her master's degree in secondary school science education from Columbia University Teachers College.

Mrs. Cobb has taught general science and physical science to junior high school students at Rye High School, Rye, New York, and at the Manhattan Day School in New York City. She is the mother of two children and the author of several books for young people, most of them on scientific subjects.